11-25-73

THE CHARITY

OF

NATIONS

THE POLITICAL ECONOMY
OF INTERNATIONAL RELATIONS
SERIES
Edited by Benjamin J. Cohen

POWER AND WEALTH
The Political Economy of International Power
by Klaus Knorr

THE CHARITY OF NATIONS
The Political Economy of Foreign Aid
by David Wall

FORTHCOMING *

THE POLITICAL ECONOMY OF IMPERIALISM
by Benjamin J. Cohen

THE POLITICAL ECONOMY OF
ECONOMIC GROWTH AND INTERNATIONAL CHANGE
by Robert G. Gilpin

THE POLITICAL ECONOMY OF INTERNATIONAL TRADE
by William H. Branson

THE POLITICAL ECONOMY OF
INTERNATIONAL COMMUNIST RELATIONS
by Franklyn D. Holzman

* All book titles are tentative.

THE CHARITY

OF

NATIONS

THE POLITICAL ECONOMY
OF FOREIGN AID

BY

DAVID WALL

Basic Books, Inc., Publishers

NEW YORK

EDITOR'S PREFACE

Benjamin J. Cohen

This volume is the second of the Basic Books series on the political economy of international relations. The series is designed to fill a serious gap in the modern, conventional literature on international relations—a gap which exists between the disciplines of economics and political science. For the most part, economists writing about international economics tend to ignore the political aspects of their subject. Struggles for power and conflicts of interest are either ignored or assumed away, or else they are dismissed as "irrational" aberrations in the behavior of economic man. Conversely, most political scientists writing about international politics tend to ignore the economic aspects of their subject. Considerations of welfare and resource allocation hardly ever seem to figure importantly in any of their discussions. Only a few lonely scholars seem prepared to combine and integrate both aspects of international relations within a single analytical framework.

That the two ought to be so combined and integrated cannot be doubted. They are certainly combined and integrated in the dynamics of the real world. Much of what passes for international politics is, in fact, concern with economic issues; much of what concerns international economists is, in fact, politics. For students of international relations, there is an urgent need to comprehend both the economics and the politics of their field. In short, there is an urgent need for a proper *political economy* of international relations.

This series is meant to help meet that need. Each volume is intended to focus on the political economy of a single topic under the broad heading of international relations. Each will examine both economic and political aspects at length and in considerable detail. Each will be designed to provide supplementary readings in courses on international economics or international politics.

The topic examined in the present volume is foreign aid. Few topics in international relations are more obviously candidates for integrated political-economic analysis. Foreign aid necessarily has implications for the economic welfare of both donor and recipient countries. It influences levels of income, productivity, and investment; it alters growth rates and the distribution of the world's resources. Yet it also necessarily involves political considerations, both at the domestic level and at the level of intercountry relations. No complete and comprehensive treatment of the topic can afford to leave out any of these important aspects.

David Wall's volume does not. Quite the contrary, Wall successfully addresses himself to virtually all of the important aspects of foreign aid. What is aid? What are the motives of donor governments in sponsoring such programs? What are the domestic and international political implications? What are the domestic and international economic implications? How does one determine how much aid is needed, or to whom it should be distributed, or how? These and related issues are all carefully evaluated by this experienced expert in the field. Wall, like any individual, is not without his own preferences and opinions. But from the very beginning he deliberately makes his attitudes and biases explicit, in order to clarify the bases for many of his subsequent conclusions and judgments. Readers may perhaps wish to question some of his normative value judgments; that is only natural in debates of public issues such as this. But they will hardly find grounds for questioning the objectivity or professional quality of the basic analysis itself. This volume should quickly come to be regarded as a significant new contribution to the literature on foreign aid.

PREFACE

The subject matter of aid and the literature surrounding it are vast, as I discovered when engaged in the research on which this book is based. I have been very selective in choosing issues for inclusion in this volume, which is intended as an introduction for college students and laymen. I include and emphasize those issues which I consider to be important and worthy of attention, and include also Suggestions for Further Reading which contains references to authors of widely different views to balance my own biases. Many people assisted me in many ways in the production of this book. To all of them I extend my thanks, and if the reader finds this book useful, so must he. Two people must be singled out for special mention: Benjamin J. Cohen and John White. Also, John Karlick, Timothy King, and James Grant provided me with introductions to several people in Washington, D.C., who made useful suggestions and stimulated many ideas in my mind. My wife, Nancy, who read the manuscript, made many valuable recommendations and provided editorial, secretarial, and dogsbody services above and beyond the call of duty. Without her help and the sometimes puzzled tolerance of my children, Edmund, Shane, and Deborah, the book would never have been finished.

DAVID WALL

University of Sussex, England
1973

CONTENTS

THE CHARITY

OF

NATIONS

I

INTRODUCTION

I am always suspicious of books which begin with a definition, as too often it is simply the author arbitrarily restricting the scope of his analysis. In the case of this book, however, an opening definition is necessary as the key word in the book's subtitle has been used haphazardly in recent years. The word "aid" in this book refers to government-sponsored flows of resources made available on concessional terms to foreign governments, either directly on a bilateral basis or indirectly via multilateral organizations. This is a fairly wide definition. Only resource flows which are commercially determined are excluded from coverage. Yet the reader would be well-advised to remain suspicious. Even if he is satisfied that he now knows what I mean by aid he should remember that political economy is not a science. There is no body of accepted knowledge which can be used to explain the various aspects of actual aid programs and which can be tested against the facts. To put this another way, there is no such thing as *the* political economy of aid.

Political economy involves the systematic (and hopefully explicit) expression of political bias concerning economic factors at play in given environments. On the one hand this entails a process of prescription and proscription derived from a particular political viewpoint. And on the other hand it involves the analysis of such prescriptions and proscriptions in order to uncover and examine the political viewpoints they express. Many of my colleagues would disagree with such a description of political economy and would argue that it simply involves economists taking into account the political factors which are present in the environments in which they operate. The catch lies in the phrase "taking into account." I believe I am being more realistic when I say that there are as many varieties of political economy as there are political viewpoints. The point of this discussion is to warn the reader that I am not politically neutral and to indicate to him my own particular systematic bias.

As a political animal I regard aid as a good thing, the more the better. As an economist by profession I am concerned with seeing that aid is used as efficiently as possible. These two seemingly simple statements beg many questions, the most obvious being what do I mean by a "good thing," and by "efficiently." By a "good thing," I mean that being aware that many of my fellow human beings live in a state of acute distress and believing that aid can contribute to the alleviation of such distress, I am in favor of as much aid as possible being made available to those who need it. As an economist I instinctively add the rider "and can use it efficiently" to that last sentence, using the word "efficiently" in the sense that for a given amount of aid the amount of distress alleviated should be maximized. I want to make it absolutely clear at this stage that the objective I see aid contributing toward is the reduction and eventual elimination of human misery. *Yet it is not at all clear how such misery can be removed.* Most works on aid treat it as an instrument to be used for producing something they call "development."

When people talk about "developing" or "less developed" countries, the implication is that they know what it is the developing countries are moving toward and that they regard such a process as desirable.[1] Yet many forms of economic change involve increased human misery and distress. Few economists have

---

[1] In this book the descriptions "poor," "less developed," "developing," are used to describe the countries in the Third World.

concerned themselves with the question: "what is development?" Those who have give answers such as increases in the amount of total income generated in the manufacturing sector; increases in total income; increases in the use of one or several "modern" items such as telephones, bricks, cement, electricity, roads, or high protein foods; or most commonly, increases in per capita income. It is, however, possible for a country to progress on all these points simultaneously and yet for the total amount of human distress found within it to increase too; witness South Africa and Pakistan (readers with different viewpoints might prefer to use China, Russia, and Cuba as examples).

The average reader will by now think that I am in the process of painting myself into a corner; the more sophisticated will say that I am in danger of getting into an infinite regress. So let me say quickly that although economists do not know what the average man requires to be happy, we can identify certain things which make him miserable. Aid is powerless to remove some sources of misery, for example, torture and murder. But it can contribute to the removal of others such as hunger, illness, lack of clothing, and homelessness. The processes involved in using domestic resources to combat such sources of misery is properly the subject matter of economists. When such processes are augmented by transfers on concessional terms of resources from abroad, we enter the realms of the political economy of aid.

The existence of a supply of and demand for aid-financed resource flows implies that market forces (as controlled domestically by governments) do not produce a global distribution of resources which is desirable to either donor or recipient countries. At this stage it does not matter why such a distribution would be undesirable to either side; all that matters is that it could be. The result is the emergence of a policy of redistribution of resources from rich countries to poor countries parallel to the redistribution that takes place within most countries from rich to poor citizens. Such redistribution results in some people being worse off and in others being better off, in the sense that their command over resources which they can use to remove some causes of their misery decreases or increases. It should now become clear that I have written this Introduction on such a personal level because *I* want to argue that *the tax burden imposed on rich countries in order to sustain their aid programs involves a sacrifice in welfare which is less than the potential gain in welfare which the less-developed countries derive from such programs*. This is my political judgment.

It will be seen in the chapters which follow that assessing the costs and benefits of aid programs is no easy task. One problem, for example, derives from the tendency to personify countries according to their mean per capita income. Thus, people tend to see the United States of America in the person of, say, a white middle-class family of four living in a split-level home in the suburbs, possessing two cars and all modern kitchen equipment and household gadgets. Similarly, in most cases people see a country such as Ecuador in the guise of a peasant family of six or seven whose pitiful income is derived from weeding in a banana plantation and growing potatoes on a small, rocky Andean plot. With such a contrast in mind it is easy to think that $10 in tax transferred from the American family to the Indian peasant represents a gain in the total welfare of the two families. It would be less clear-cut if we compared a fatherless black family in the ghettos of Chicago with a plantation owner in Ecuador. Clearly then, in order to hold to the political judgment I made in the last paragraph, I have to assume that the aid programs of the rich countries are sustained by taxes on the incomes of people who are rich by international standards. I also have to assume that aid funds are used to improve the lot of the poorer sections of the world community. Insuring that these assumptions actually operate is one of the major problems of aid administrations in the donor countries.

Aid, then, is government-enforced international income redistribution. The donor governments seek to convince their electorates to support the government's positions on such questions as why aid is necessary, how much is needed (i.e. at least as much as they already give), who should receive aid, how it should be used, how its use should be controlled, what form it should take, and the prospects for its efficient use. The discussion of questions such as these is the purpose of this book. Chapter 2 describes the evolution of the aid programs of the donor countries since 1945, and Chapter 3 discusses the motives of donor country governments in sponsoring such programs. Chapter 4 is concerned with public attitudes toward aid, not only with how the average taxpayer thinks about his country's aid program, but also with politicians' attempts to influence him. The impact, on the attitudes of the public and of politicians, derived from the activities of various interest groups and lobbies is estimated. This chapter also describes the legislative process followed in the largest donor country—the United States—in drawing up its aid program. Chapter 5 is addressed to the question of how much aid less-developed countries need. Much attention has been given to this question in international circles in recent years. The answers arrived at as a result of such discussion, such as 0.7 percent or 1 percent of the Gross National Product of the rich countries, are purely arbitrary and have no economic validity. The only valid answer is "it all depends." Chapter 5 discusses the many factors on which it depends.

Many of the controversies over aid concern the form it should take. People have ranked themselves on either side of many dichotomies on this issue, of which two examples are the questions of whether aid should be given away or only loaned and of whether aid should be used to finance identifiable projects or should be given in the form of open checks to finance overall economic programs. Chapter 6 presents an account of these and other dichotomies and analyzes the arguments put forward on both sides of the debates. One dichotomy—should aid be channeled via bilateral or multilateral agencies?—has gained such prominence in the debates over aid that it has a complete chapter devoted to it—Chapter 7. At the forefront of the bilateral/multilateral debate are the issues of political interference in aid relationships, relative operational efficiency, and of who should have the right to control the use of aid. These issues are all taken up in Chapter 7.

Finally, although the topic is touched on in previous chapters, Chapter 8 takes up the question of the distribution of aid, i.e. of how the total amount of aid available should be distributed among the poor countries. It looks at criteria which have been proposed as guides for determining aid distribution and concludes that there is no objective or scientific method of measuring a poor country's "need" for aid.

II

THE STRUCTURE OF
WESTERN AID PROGRAMS

Introduction: The Evolution of Western Aid Programs

Western aid has two origins: [1] U.S. fear of communist expansionism and European imperial politics. The U.S. aid program effectively began with the Marshall Plan, which was directed to the reconstruction of Europe and Japan. The intention of the Marshall Plan was to provide the United States with a first line of defense against possible Russian aggression. The only other significant "aid" programs in this period immediately following World War II were those of France and Great Britain and, to a lesser extent, the Netherlands, Belgium, and Portugal. This European aid simply reflected the financial cost of maintaining empires in Africa, Asia, and the Pacific and Caribbean regions. As the reconstruction of Europe and Japan progressed and the European countries' empires began to disintegrate, new independent political entities emerged and the Western powers,

[1] This discussion of the evolution of Western aid programs is necessarily brief. The reader who requires a more complete history of aid is referred to G. Ohlin, *Foreign Aid Policies Reconsidered* (Paris: Development Center of the Organization for Economic Cooperation and Development, 1966).

especially the United States, began to shift the emphasis of their aid efforts.

The shift in U.S. aid, following the enactment of the Mutual Security Act in 1952, reflected a fairly straightforward extension of Cold War containment policy from Western to Southern Europe and to Asia. The successful communist revolution in China, the Korean War, and the diminution of British and French power and influence in Burma and Indo-China strengthened the arguments of those in favor of such a shift of emphasis. By the mid-fifties the bulk of U.S. aid was going to poorer countries on the periphery of the communist bloc: Greece, Turkey, Burma, South Vietnam, Taiwan, and South Korea. The aid provided by the United States to the countries of the Third World was never, however, on the scale of that provided to Europe and Japan under the Marshall Plan. Marshall Plan aid accounted for 2 percent of the U.S. Gross National Product (GNP) in 1949, while development aid has never reached as much as 1 percent.

Concurrent with the shift in emphasis of U.S. aid was the growth of European aid programs. Initially provided by imperial and ex-imperial powers to colonies and ex-colonies, the programs grew and diversified as a result of U.S. pressure on Europe to assume an increasing share of the "burden" of providing aid to the Third World. The U.S. share of total Western aid fell from around two thirds in the late fifties to less than half by the late sixties. Nevertheless, the U.S. aid program continued to dominate the Western aid effort, both in financial terms and in the field of technical assistance. The objectives of U.S. aid—the promotion of political stability in the Third World, the prevention of the spread of Russian and Chinese influence, and the creation of a more prosperous environment for the world in general—were seen by Americans as being of benefit not only to themselves but also to their Western allies. The United States naturally expected that the countries which it had helped to reconstruct should join with it in sharing the burden of what it felt to be a growing need for aid in the Third World.

With the creation (on U.S. initiative) of the Development

Assistance Group (DAG) of Western donor countries in 1960, a serious attempt was made to collect data on the aid programs of the Western countries. This data collection activity was taken over by the successor to the DAG, the Development Assistance Committee (DAC) of the Organization for Economic Cooperation and Development (OECD), when it was established in 1961. The establishment of DAC has led to an increase in the quantity and quality of data available on the aid programs of Western countries. The rest of this chapter is devoted to a summary and analysis of some of these data. The realities of the situation are, however, highly complex. In order to build up a reasonably accurate picture of the growth and structure of aid programs, many different aspects of the situation must be examined. The crude data must be looked at in the light of the conditions under which aid programs operate, conditions which frequently distort the effects of the aid.

The Size and Costs of the Aid Programs

Table 2–1 shows data on the size of total net Official Development Assistance (ODA) provided by DAC members in 1970, 1965, and 1960. An indicative but not strictly comparable figure for annual averages of the net flows of official financial resources over the period 1956–1959 is also shown. ODA is defined as concessionary flows of resources from donor government sources to less-developed countries (loosely defined), and multilateral agencies. The figures in Table 2–1 represent the budgetary allocations of ODA, which were actually disbursed (as against simply promised) in each of the years, net of repayments (but not interest) on past loans. While the data of Table 2–1 illustrate the overall *financial* size and distribution of the aid programs of DAC members, they say little or nothing about the size and distribution of the *economic* cost involved in maintaining them.

Donor countries see their aid programs as constituting a burden. They have tended to regard the sort of data shown in Table 2–1 as indicating the absolute burden of their own aid programs

TABLE 2-1

Official Development Assistance
The Net Flow of Official Development Assistance to Less-Developed
Countries and Multilateral Agencies, 1970, 1965, 1960, and 1956–1959

(Disbursements Net of Repayments on Past Loans in Millions of U.S. Dollars)

COUNTRY	1970		1965		1960		ANNUAL AVERAGE 1956–1959	
	AMOUNT	RANK	AMOUNT	RANK	AMOUNT	RANK	AMOUNT	RANK
United States	3,050	1	3,418	1	2,702	1	2,207	1
France	951	2	752	2	823	2	796	2
Germany	599	3	456	4	223	4	254	4
Japan	458	4	244	5	105	5	124	5
United Kingdom	447	5	472	3	407	3	273	3
Canada	346	6	96	8	75	8	58	7
Australia	203	7	119	6	59	9	43	8
Netherlands	196	8	70	9	35	11	36	9
Italy	147	9	60	10	77	7	91	6
Belgium	120	10	102	7	101	6	36	9
Sweden	117	11	38	11	7	12	9	11
Denmark	59	12	13	14	5	13	6	12
Norway	37	13	11	16	5	13	6	12
Switzerland	30	14	12	15	4	14	13	10
Portugal	29	15	22	13	37	10	6	12
Austria	19	16	31	12	na [1]	—	2	13
Total DAC Member Countries Combined	6,808		5,916		4,665		3,959 [2]	

Source: *Development Assistance: Efforts and Policies of the Members of the Development Assistance Committee 1970 and 1971 Reviews*, OECD, Paris 1970–1971. Annex Table 2 (Hereafter DAC reviews are referred to as DAC Review 1970, 1971, etc.).

[1] na = not available.
[2] The data for 1956–1959 are not strictly comparable with that for later years.

and their relative burden vis-à-vis the programs of other donors. Much effort has been expended in attempts to determine what constitutes an acceptable overall aid burden for rich countries and to define an equitable distribution of such a burden among themselves. However, the apparent burden of aid, as indicated by the figures in Table 2–1, is very different from the real economic burden; to get a clear idea of this real burden, or "true" cost of aid, many additional factors must be taken into consideration. This and the next 3 sections of this chapter will examine these additional factors.

First, it is necessary to take account of inflation. The annual rate of growth in total DAC aid over the decade 1961 to 1970 was 3 percent. This rate of growth is not much more than the rate of price inflation in DAC countries over the same period. In other words, the amounts of real resources represented by the sums referred to in the table have, on average, grown much more slowly than the figures suggest. Vis-à-vis some aid-financed resources, such as technical assistance and advice, real amounts have fallen considerably.

There is, therefore, only one definite conclusion which we can draw from Table 2–1. This is that as the aid programs of DAC members other than the United States have increased in financial terms (in some cases quite markedly), the share of the total amount of DAC aid contributed by the United States has fallen, from 56 percent in the period 1956–1959 to 45 percent in 1970.

Even if we take the data in Table 2–1 to represent the true financial *cost* of aid we still do not know how much of a burden was each donor's contribution. "Burden" is a relative term, and just as the burden imposed on a carrier by a given weight depends on his physical strength, so does the burden of a given amount of aid contributed depend on the economic strength of the donor. One conventional measure of a country's economic strength is its GNP. Hence, taking the percentage of a country's GNP allocated to its aid program is one way of measuring the burden it represents. Table 2–2 shows the percentage of its GNP which each DAC member's official development assistance program constituted in the years 1970, 1965, and 1960, with the average for all DAC countries in those years. Comparing Tables 2–1 and 2–2 we can see that although total aid has increased, the burden it has placed on the donors has fallen substantially over the period. This is because the combined GNP of DAC countries

TABLE 2–2

The Net Flow of Official Development Assistance
in Relation to Gross National Product,[1] 1970, 1965, and 1960

(Disbursements Net of Repayments on Past Loans: Percentages and Rank)

COUNTRY	1970		1965		1960	
	SHARE OF GNP	RANK	SHARE OF GNP	RANK	SHARE OF GNP	RANK
France	0.65	1	0.75	2	1.38	2
Netherlands	0.63	2	0.36	8	0.31	8
Australia	0.59	3	0.52	4	0.38	6
Belgium	0.48	4	0.59	3	0.88	3
Portugal	0.45	5	1.59	1	1.45	1
Canada	0.43	6	0.19	11	0.19	11
Denmark	0.38	7	0.13	13	0.09	13
United Kingdom	0.37	8	0.47	6	0.56	4
Sweden	0.37	8	0.19	11	0.05	14
Norway	0.33	9	0.16	12	0.11	12
Germany	0.32	10	0.40	7	0.33	7
United States	0.31	11	0.49	5	0.53	5
Japan	0.23	12	0.28	10	0.24	9
Italy	0.16	13	0.10	14	0.22	10
Switzerland	0.14	14	0.08	15	0.04	15
Austria	0.13	15	0.34	9	na	—
Total DAC Countries	0.34		0.44		0.52	

Source: DAC Review, 1971. Annex Table 9.
[1] At market prices.

has increased faster than their combined aid flows. This is clearly indicated by the fall in the figure for aid as a percentage of GNP from 0.52 percent in 1960 to 0.34 percent in 1970. Although this overall fall is largely due to the dominating effect of the fall in the U.S. figure from 0.53 percent to 0.31 percent over the same period, it is interesting to note how the figures for all donors have tended to converge around the average of 0.34 percent. Thus, in 1961 (the peak year for the average), the average percentage of the share of GNP accounted for by aid in those countries below the average was 0.21 percent and for those above the average it was 1.00 percent; the comparable figures in 1970 were 0.23 percent and 0.48 percent, respectively. Thus, statistically speaking, relative burdens are converging about a declining trend. Another interesting feature illustrated by this table is that the burden of aid borne by those countries which emerged from World War II with colonial empires intact has declined: for Belgium the figure falls from 0.88 percent in 1960 to 0.48 percent in 1970; for France, from 1.38 to 0.65; for Portugal, from 1.45 to 0.45; and for the United Kingdom, from 0.56 to 0.37. Finally, it should be noted that the "new" countries (Australia and Canada), and the Scandinavian countries, significantly increased the amount of funds they allocated to their aid programs.

Grants, Loans, and the Terms of Aid

Both the cost and the value of an aid program depend to a large extent on the forms the aid takes and the terms on which it is offered. For this reason, the concept of burden on which Table 2–2 is based is totally inadequate. It assumes that all components of the flows of ODA given in Table 2–1 involve an equal sacrifice to the donors. This is not the case. The economic cost to a donor of giving aid which will never be repaid—i.e. a grant—is obviously greater than the economic cost of providing it in the form of loans which will be repaid. Unfortunately no data are available on the proportion of actual disbursements, shown in Table 2–1, which took the form of grants. A comparable figure for the grant proportion of aid *commitments*—amounts *promised* by donors in a given year—is, however, available. (The difference between disbursements and commitments is due partly to accounting conventions and partly to delays in offers of aid being taken up.)

The data for 1970 are shown in column one of Table 2–3. We can see from this table that the donors who gave most of their ODA in grant form were Norway (99 percent) and Bel-

TABLE 2–3

*Grant Element of Official Development Assistance Commitments
Made in 1970*

	1	2	3
		ODA	
	GRANTS AS A	COMMITMENTS AS	GRANTS AS
	PERCENTAGE OF	PERCENTAGE OF	PERCENTAGE OF
COUNTRY	ODA	GNP	GNP (COLS. 1×2)
Australia	91	0.68	0.62
Austria	41	0.16	0.07
Belgium	92	0.58	0.53
Canada	65	0.51	0.33
Denmark	92	0.40	0.37
France	73	0.84	0.61
Germany	54	0.44	0.24
Italy	54	0.21	0.11
Japan	39	0.30	0.12
Netherlands	64	0.66	0.42
Norway	99	0.37	0.37
Portugal	27	1.09	0.29
Sweden	82	0.69	0.57
Switzerland	82	0.18	0.15
United Kingdom	50	0.44	0.22
United States	64	0.34	0.22
Total DAC	63	0.41	0.26

Source: DAC Review, 1971. Annex Table 11.

gium, while at the other end of the scale Portugal and Japan
extended, respectively, 27 percent and 39 percent of their ODA
in the form of grants.

It can be argued that as loans are extended with the expecta-
tion of being repaid, only grants should be counted as *real*
aid. In this case the cost of aid—or burden it imposes on the
donors—should be measured by the proportion of GNP which
is given away directly in the form of grants to poor countries.
To provide a basis for comparison, the data on ODA *commitments* (made by DAC members in 1970), as a percentage of
the GNPs of donors in 1970, are shown in column two of Table
2–3. These percentages are greater than those based on ODA
disbursements. By multiplying the figures in column one by

those in column two we can arrive at data on the ratio of grants of ODA to the GNP of the donors in percentage terms; this data is given in column three. Thus if we count as aid only the grants in the ODA of the DAC members, then these donors committed themselves to giving away only 0.26 percent of their combined GNP in 1970. The total commitments counted by donors themselves as ODA were, by way of contrast, equal to 0.41 percent of their combined GNP. The reader should note that using the grant concept of aid means that the "burden" relationships among the donors change significantly. The most notable change in the ranking is the fall of Portugal from first place to ninth; other significant changes in rankings are those for Australia, Denmark, and Norway, whose positions change from fourth to first, tenth to joint sixth, and eleventh to joint sixth, respectively.

Donor countries argue that most of the loans they make to less-developed countries are made on terms (with respect to interest charges and repayment conditions) more favorable than those less-developed countries could obtain in the open market. Some claim that in order to make loans to less-developed countries, rich countries have to forgo present consumption and replace it with consumption in the future from the income streams created by interest and repayment receipts.

Consumption *now* is generally preferred to consumption in the future. It is argued, therefore, that the difference between the donors' valuation of the present consumption, which could have been paid for with the money used for aid, and the future consumption, which will be paid for by the receipts of interest and capital repayments, should be regarded as the equivalent of a grant. This "grant equivalent" of a loan may be regarded as a "cost" to donors, to be counted as part of the economic burden involved in maintaining an aid program. Much effort has been expended in recent years on calculations and comparisons of the grant equivalent of, or grant element in, loans with different interest rates and repayment terms. Most are based on the notion of *discounting* future income to reflect the fact that a given amount of resources is worth more today, to borrowers and lenders alike, than the value of a promise today of the same amount sometime in the future.

In its annual review of the aid programs of its members, DAC calculates the grant element of the loan component of ODA from the point of view of recipients. These calculations are based on a discount rate of 10 percent. This assumes that recipients regard the cost of repaying, or paying a given sum of interest charges on, a given loan in one year's time as 10 percent less of a burden than they would one which would have to be repaid now. For a given rate of discount, the grant element of a loan is greater the lower is the rate of interest, the greater the period over which it has to be repaid, and the longer any grace period before repayments are due. Thus, using a rate of discount of 10 percent, loans for 10 years at 2 percent, 5 percent, and 7 percent interests with grace periods of 5 years would have grant elements of 41.8 percent, 26.1 percent, and 15.7 percent, respectively. If these loans had been made for 20 years with nothing else changed the grant elements would increase to 54.9 percent, 34.2 percent, and 21.6 percent. Similarly, if the grace period on the 20-year loans were increased to 10 years the grant element in 2, 5, and 7 percent interest loans would further increase to 61.4, 38.4, and 23.0 percent, respectively.[2]

Table 2–4 gives data on the average terms of ODA commitments given by DAC members in 1970. It shows also, in column four, the grant element of these commitments as calculated by DAC. Column five shows the total grant element in ODA commitments in 1970—i.e. grants plus the grant element in loans —and column six shows this total grant element as a proportion of DAC members' GNPs in 1970. The average grant element of total ODA *commitments* by DAC members in 1970 is given as 0.34 percent. ODA *commitments* by DAC members in 1970 were

---

[2] The examples are taken from Annex Tables 1 and 2, Ohlin, *Foreign Aid Policies Reconsidered*. A further discussion of the concept of grant element is given there.

valued (net of repayments) at $8,144.6 million. This was 20 percent greater than the equivalent figure for ODA *disbursements*, which was $6,808.0 million. If we assume that the terms of the loan component of the disbursement were the same on average as those of the commitments, then the grant element of actual flows (disbursements) of ODA in 1970 would be equal to *only 0.27 percent* of the combined GNP of the DAC countries.

The general conclusion of this analysis is that the cost, in terms of resources given away, to the DAC members of maintaining their aid programs is considerably less than the crude

TABLE 2–4

Average Terms and Grant Element of
Official Development Commitments in 1970

COUNTRY	LOANS WEIGHTED AVERAGES			GRANT ELEMENT OF LOANS AS PERCENT OF LOAN COMMITMENTS	TOTAL GRANT ELEMENT AS PERCENT OF TOTAL ODA COMMITMENTS	TOTAL GRANT ELEMENT OF ODA AS PERCENT OF GNP [1]
	PERIOD OF LOANS (YEARS)	INTEREST RATE PERCENT	GRACE PERIOD (YEARS)			
	1	2	3	4	5	6
Australia	14.0	6.4	4.0	20	93	0.63
Austria	13.9	5.1	4.2	28	58	0.09
Belgium	29.6	2.3	9.2	64	97	0.56
Canada	48.5	0.2	9.8	89	96	0.49
Denmark	25.0	0.0	7.0	77	98	0.39
France	16.2	3.7	2.3	37	83	0.70
Germany	27.5	2.9	8.5	57	80	0.35
Italy	13.1	4.9	5.2	31	68	0.14
Japan	21.4	3.7	6.7	47	67	0.20
Netherlands	29.0	2.9	7.8	57	85	0.56
Norway	23.0	2.4	9.0	59	99	0.37
Portugal	29.0	4.0	8.0	49	63	0.69
Sweden	35.4	1.5	10.0	73	95	0.66
Switzerland	36.0	2.0	8.0	67	94	0.17
United Kingdom	24.6	1.7	6.2	63	82	0.36
United States	37.4	2.6	8.7	63	87	0.30
Total DAC	29.9	2.8	7.4	57	84	0.34

Source: DAC Review, 1971. Text Tables IV–2 and IV–1.

[1] Column 6 was arrived at by multiplying Column 5 of this table by Column 2 of Table 2–3.

figures suggest. With reference to specific countries, we can see that figures in Table 2–1 on absolute amounts of aid disbursed are misleading. When allowance is made for "ability to bear the burden" of aid and the grant component of the crude figures, the ranking of countries by apparent burdens changes, in some cases considerably. Thus although the United States is the largest donor in absolute terms, it is twelfth out of sixteen when ranked by the size of burden involved, as measured by the grant element of its aid as a proportion of its GNP. Only Japan, Switzerland, Italy, and Austria make less effort in these terms. If we call the grant element of ODA "real" aid, then U.S. aid is equivalent to less than one-third of one cent per dollar of its Gross National Product. None of the DAC members gives away in aid as much as three-quarters of one cent per dollar of their GNPs. On average they give about one-third of one cent per dollar. It is difficult to see how such flows can be considered to be burdens.

The Effect of Tied Aid

As the aid programs of donor countries expanded during the 1960s, so did the practice of tying aid to the procurement of goods and services in the donor country. The reasoning behind this was that tying aid would allow donors to reduce further the burden of their aid programs. The reasoning was faulty, but the effects on poor countries—reducing the value to them of receipts of aid—were real. Forcing aid recipients to spend their aid receipts in the donor country prevents the forces of market competition from operating efficiently and allows firms in donor countries to benefit from monopoly pricing.

Obviously if a company gives you $100,000 credit on condition that you buy its machines and then charges you $1,000 each for machines which are normally priced at $800, the real cost to the company of the deal is considerably reduced: it has to provide only 100 machines instead of 125. The price recipients have to pay for tied aid-financed purchases can be above the world market prices of the commodities concerned for a variety of reasons. For example, much U.S. tied aid is spent on purchases of U.S. steel products, which are priced above world market levels because the U.S. steel industry is protected from foreign competition. Also, it frequently happens that when a monopolistic supplier in a donor country is approached for products to be financed by his country's aid agency, he raises his prices because he knows that the recipient country has no choice but to buy his products. Another price-raising practice is the condition that aid-financed purchases from a donor country must be transported to the recipient by donor-owned shipping lines. This puts such shipping companies in a monopoly position and they are able to—and do—raise their charges for such freight above free market levels. Aid literature abounds with examples of such overpricing, frequently indicating prices 20 percent to 50 percent above world market levels.[3]

Donor governments do not publish systematic tabulations of the price effects of aid tying. This makes it impossible to assess correctly the cost of their aid-tying practices. All it is possible to say, in general, is that, as argued above, the crude financial data of DAC members' aid programs overestimate their financial burden by some 20 percent. If allowance were made for the price effects of aid tying, taking typical figures of 20 percent and 50 percent of overpricing, then the real cost of their combined aid effort would appear to be reduced to between one-quarter and one-sixth of 1 percent of their combined GNPs.

The Mounting Debt Problem

Although the terms of ODA loans have been easing in recent years with a trend toward lower interest rates and longer repayment periods, the proportion of loans in ODA has been increasing. As Table 2–5 shows, the bilateral grant proportion of total ODA has fallen from 74 percent in 1962 to 48 percent

[3] See, for example, Chapter 10, "The Tying of Aid" in J. Bhagwati and R. Eckaus, eds. *Foreign Aid* (London: Penguin Books, 1970).

TABLE 2–5

Shares of Total Official Aid Disbursements from DAC Members Going As Flows to Multilateral Agencies and As Bilateral Grants: 1962–1970

	1962	1963	1964	1965	1966	1967	1968	1969	1970
Flows to Multilateral Agencies, Percent	9	6	6	6	5	11	11	15	17
Bilateral Grants, Percent [1]	74	69	64	64	62	55	53	50	48

Source: DAC Review. Various issues.

[1] These figures differ from those in Table 2–3 as the data there are in terms of *commitments* while those in this table concern *disbursements*.

TABLE 2–6

The Debt Structure of Eight Less-Developed Countries in 1968

COUNTRY	DEBT OUTSTANDING AS OF JANUARY 1, 1968 (DISBURSED ONLY): IN MILLIONS OF DOLLARS	DEBT SERVICE PAYMENTS				ANNUAL AVERAGE NET RECEIPTS OF OFFICIAL AID 1967–1969: IN MILLIONS OF DOLLARS
		MILLIONS OF DOLLARS	AS A PERCENTAGE OF TOTAL DEBT OUTSTANDING	OF WHICH		
				AMORTIZATION PERCENTAGE	INTEREST PERCENTAGE	
	1	2	3	4	5	6
Mexico	2,162	626	28.9	22.3	6.6	117
Argentina	1,781	478	26.9	20.8	6.1	−20
India	5,604 [1]	357	6.4	3.7	2.7	1,072
Chile	1,117	171	15.4	11.5	3.9	179
Colombia	796	102	12.7	9.2	3.5	147
Tunisia	416	60	14.5	11.1	3.4	100
Morocco	481 [2]	48	10.8	6.6	4.2	89
Nigeria	403 [2]	41	10.2	6.5	3.7	106

Source: DAC Review, 1970. Text Table III–5 and Annex Table 19.

[1] As of April 1, 1968.
[2] As of July 1, 1968.

in 1970. This underplays the dominating role of loans in aid, however, for although much of the contribution of DAC members to multilateral institutions is in the form of grants, these institutions pass a large proportion of their funds on to poor countries in the form of loans. As total aid flows have increased, this has created problems for recipients. Every time a loan is made to a poor country (whether under an aid program or as part of a commercial transaction), its total debt is increased. Very little information is publicly available concerning this debt for all poor countries, but such information as we have indicates that it is increasing at an accelerating rate and that the terms are on average getting more stringent. With total aid now leveling off and the loan proportion increasing, and as past loans become due for repayment or servicing, the proportion of new aid which less-developed countries have to earmark for such payments is increasing. We do have detailed data for eight poor countries' debt positions in 1968. Table 2–6 gives data on total outstanding debt (with respect to official aid *and* commercial transactions) for these countries and also the figures for the cost of amortization and interest charges on their debt. The last column shows the average annual net receipt of official aid by these countries over the period 1967–1969. As the aid figures are net of amortization and as column two includes interest on official nonconcessionary loans and private flows, the data are not strictly comparable: the error is probably of the order of 3 to 4 percent. Allowing for this error, we can still get a reasonable picture of the degree to which new official aid simply represented the donor countries returning funds to themselves as payments on past loans.

It is clear from Table 2–6 that the debt position of less-developed countries varies enormously. For some countries, even after allowing for inaccuracies in the data, aid receipts were substantially less than the payments which they have to make annually on their debts to the rich countries. At the other end of the scale, aid to India was three times the debt service charges. On the basis of different data the World Bank has calculated what it calls the aggregate *net transfer* of external resources to 80 less-developed countries over the period

TABLE 2-7

External Resource Flows and Service Payments on External Public and Publicly Guaranteed Debt, Eighty Developing Countries (In Millions of Dollars) [1]

	1965	1966	1967	1968	1969
Gross Flow	8,774	8,355	9,788	10,324	10,153
Debt Service	3,416	3,787	3,978	4,528	4,968
Net Transfer	5,358	4,568	5,810	5,796	5,185

Source: World Bank International Development Association, *Annual Report* 1971, Annex Table 9. As quoted in UNCTAD Document Number TD/B/C.3/92. *The Flow of Financial Resources*. Geneva, 1971.

[1] The African countries are: Botswana, Burundi, Cameroon, Central African Republic, Chad, Democratic Republic of Congo (Zaire), Dahomey, Ethiopia, Gabon, Ghana, Guinea, Ivory Coast, Kenya, Lesotho, Liberia, Malagasy Republic, Malawi, Mali, Mauritius, Mauritania, Morocco, Niger, Nigeria, Rhodesia, Rwanda, Senegal, Sierra Leone, Somalia, Sudan, Swaziland, United Republic of Tanzania, Togo, Tunisia, Uganda, United Arab Republic, Upper Volta, Zambia.
The Asian countries are: Afghanistan, Ceylon, Taiwan, India, Indonesia, Republic of Korea, Malaysia, Pakistan, Philippines, Singapore, Thailand.
The Middle East countries are: Iran, Iraq, Israel, Jordan, Syria.
The Western Hemisphere countries are: Argentina, Bolivia, Brazil, Chile, Colombia, Costa Rica, Dominican Republic, Ecuador, El Salvador, Guatemala, Guyana, Honduras, Jamaica, Mexico, Nicaragua, Panama, Paraguay, Peru, Trinidad and Tobago, Uruguay, Venezuela.
The Southern European countries are: Cyprus, Greece, Malta, Spain, Turkey, Yugoslavia.

1965 to 1969. By net transfer it means the sum of aid and other capital flows to poor countries *less* repayments of capital and interest. These data are given in Table 2-7. We can see that in 1969, out of a total gross inflow of capital of $10,153 million, $4,968 million (i.e. *almost half*) was sent back for servicing purposes, leaving a net transfer of $5,185 million.

As new loans are made and as the volume of outstanding debt increases (from $21.6 billion in 1961 to $59.3 billion in 1969 for the 80 countries covered in Table 2-7, according to the World Bank), so does the flow of debt servicing charges. These outflows can be seen in Table 2-7 to have increased 46 percent over the period 1965 to 1969 (from $3,416 million to $4,968 million), for the sample of poor countries covered there.

With total capital flows to poor countries tending to stabilize as the proportion of loans in it increases, it is clear that the net transfer (which can be regarded as one measure of burden to donors) of capital will continue to fall. To the poor countries the debt service charges represent an increasing burden. One way of assessing the extent of this burden is to show what proportion of a country's export receipts are required to cover its debt service charges. The secretariat of the United Nations Conference on Trade and Development (UNCTAD) have calculated this ratio for 60 less-developed countries in 1969–1970 and (on the basis of various assumptions) estimated what the ratio might look like in 1975 and 1980 (see Table 2–8).

TABLE 2–8

Debt-Service Ratios [1] and Shares of Debt-Servicing Payments, Actual and Projected, for Sixty Countries [2]

	1969–1970 [3]		1975		1980	
DEBT SERVICE RATIOS	0 TO 20	20 AND ABOVE	0 TO 20	20 AND ABOVE	0 TO 20	20 AND ABOVE
Number of Countries	55	5	52	8	43	17
Share of Group's Debt Servicing in Total Debt Servicing (Percentages)	64.9	35.1	56.4	43.4	48.2	51.8

Source: UNCTAD Document Number TD/B/C.3/96. *Liberalization and Terms and Conditions of Assistance.* Geneva, 1971.

[1] The ratio of debt-service payments to exports of goods and services.
[2] The countries covered are: Argentina, Bolivia, Brazil, Central African Republic, Ceylon, Chad, Chile, Colombia, Costa Rica, Cyprus, Dahomey, Dominican Republic, Ecuador, El Salvador, Ethiopia, Ghana, Greece, Guatemala, Guyana, Honduras, India, Indonesia, Iran, Iraq, Ivory Coast, Jamaica, Jordan, Kenya, Liberia, Malawi, Malaysia, Mauritius, Mexico, Morocco, Nicaragua, Nigeria, Pakistan, Panama, Paraguay, Peru, Philippines, Republic of Korea, Senegal, Sierra Leone, Singapore, Sudan, Syria, Taiwan, Tanzania, Thailand, Togo, Trinidad and Tobago, Tunisia, Turkey, Uganda, Uruguay, Venezuela, Yugoslavia, Zaire, and Zambia.
[3] Countries classified by their observed debt-service ratio in 1969; shares in total debt servicing based on 1970 data.

TABLE 2–9

Net Official Receipts [1]
from DAC Countries and Multilateral Agencies, 1968–1970

RECIPIENT	1 TOTAL RECEIPTS OF OFFICIAL AID ANNUAL AVERAGE FOR 1968–1970 (IN MILLIONS OF DOLLARS)	2 AID RECEIPTS PER CAPITA, BASED ON 1968 POPULATION (IN DOLLARS)
Netherlands Antilles	24	109
Surinam	21	55
Malta	17	53
Congo (Brazzaville)	282	33
South Vietnam	449	26
Laos	65	23
Tunisia	107	23
Israel	63	23
Guyana	16	23
Botswana	14	22
Jordan	46	22
Swaziland	8	21
Gabon	10	20
Fiji Islands	7	15
Chile	132	14
Singapore	26	13
Dominican Republic	52	13
Nicaragua	23	12
Jamaica	23	12
Ivory Coast	49	12
South Korea	356	12
Panama	16	11
Senegal	42	11
Liberia	13	11
Somalia	30	11
Greece	93	11
Paraguay	22	10
Hong Kong	38	10
Central African Republic	14	10
Honduras	23	9
Bolivia	41	9
Colombia	176	9
Algeria	111	9
Mauritius	6	8
Cameroon	45	8
Costa Rica	13	8
Togo	14	8

TABLE 2-9 (Continued)

Net Official Receipts [1]
from DAC Countries and Multilateral Agencies, 1968–1970

| | 1 | 2 |
| | TOTAL RECEIPTS OF OFFICIAL AID ANNUAL AVERAGE FOR 1968–1970 | AID RECEIPTS PER CAPITA, BASED ON 1968 POPULATION |
RECIPIENT	(IN MILLIONS OF DOLLARS)	(IN DOLLARS)
Gambia	3	8
Niger	29	8
Ghana	62	7
Cyprus	5	7
Morocco	104	7
Malawi	30	7
Turkey	231	7
Zambia	26	6
Kenya	69	6
Malagasy Republic	38	6
Taiwan	79	6
Trinidad and Tobago	6	6
Uruguay	16	6
Lebanon	14	5
Venezuela	52	5
Chad	19	5
Rwanda	17	5
Dahomey	13	5
Malaysia	56	5
Zaire	31	5
Barbados	1	4
Guatamala	22	4
Peru	55	4
Burundi	15	4
Ecuador	24	4
Ceylon	51	4
Philippines	140	4
Mali	19	4
Sierra-Leone	9	4
Pakistan	446	4
El Salvador	11	3
Indonesia	387	3
Tanzania	13	3
Iran	92	3
Uganda	26	3
Thailand	100	3
Mexico	140	3

TABLE 2-9 *(Continued)*

Net Official Receipts [1]
from DAC Countries and Multilateral Agencies, 1968–1970

| | 1 | 2 |
| | TOTAL RECEIPTS OF OFFICIAL AID ANNUAL AVERAGE FOR 1968–1970 | AID RECEIPTS PER CAPITA, BASED ON 1968 POPULATION |
RECIPIENT	(IN MILLIONS OF DOLLARS)	(IN DOLLARS)
Spain	86	3
Brazil	213	2
Syria	12	2
South Yemen	2	2
Cambodia	14	2
Ethiopia	46	2
India	881	2
Iraq	14	2
Nigeria	102	2
Haiti	6	1
Sudan	17	1
Burma	24	< 1
Yugoslavia	16	< 1
UAR	19	< 1
Argentina	− 3	< 0
Saudi Arabia	− 2	< 0
Rhodesia	− 3	< 0
Libya	− 3	< 0
Brunei	− 1	< 0
Kuwait	− 4	< 0
Average, all countries		4.38

Source: DAC Review, 1971. Annex Table 16.

[1] Including some nonconcessionary flows and all ODA.

Column one of Table 2–8 shows that in 1970 debt servicing charges represented more than 20 percent of the export receipts of five less-developed countries; the outflows involved being equal to 35.1 percent of the total debt servicing payments of the 60 countries in 1970. By 1975, the UNCTAD secretariat estimates, 8 of the countries will be in this category (accounting for 43.4 percent of the total outflows) and by 1980, 17, or more than a quarter of the countries covered (accounting for 51.8 percent of total outflows). This staggering debt problem should be borne in mind when reading the data given in Table 2–9, which provides an account of net receipts of aid by a selection of less-developed countries. It should, indeed, be borne in mind throughout this book.

The Distribution of Aid among Recipients

Finally, having discussed the amounts involved in DAC members' aid programs (and the questions of how much of a burden they represent to donors and of how much of a burden the servicing of the loan components is to the recipients), we turn to a brief account of the distribution of aid among recipients. The questions of "who does?" and "who should?" receive aid (and how much) are dealt with at greater length in later chapters; here our concern is with the crude data on the existing pattern of distribution. Bearing in mind the qualifications outlined in previous sections and noting that the data for the aid flows in question do not take into account payments of interest charges, we see that Table 2–9 shows the distribution of total aid among recipients. Owing to lack of comparable data, it is only possible to provide information on this basis for 94 recipients. The table gives data for average annual total, and per capita, receipts of total net official aid over the period 1968 to 1970. The aid figures (total net official aid) in this table are not strictly comparable with the data in earlier tables, as official flows not on concessional terms are included in the totals, but this does not change the overall picture significantly. In the table the countries are ranked according to per capita receipts.

The only factor which approaches a common economic characteristic of the twenty countries receiving most aid per capita is that for the most part they are relatively small in terms of population. A common political characteristic of most of these twenty is that they were until recently (and one still is) colonies of one of the donor countries. However, to be a small ex-colony is neither a guarantee of nor the only way to ensure a high ranking in the table. Clearly, defense and security factors present in

TABLE 2–10

Distribution of Net Bilateral Official Aid Receipts [1] by Political Affiliation
Annual Average for 1968–1970, in Percentages

	COMMONWEALTH COUNTRIES (EXCEPT INDIA AND PAKISTAN)	FRENCH OVERSEAS TERRITORIES AND DEPARTMENTS	OTHER FRENCH FRANC ZONE COUNTRIES IN AFRICA	LATIN AMERICAN COUNTRIES [2]	OTHER LESS-DEVELOPED COUNTRIES [3]	TOTAL TO ALL RECIPIENTS [4] (IN MILLIONS OF DOLLARS)
France	<1	33	45	– [5]	20	858
EEC Aid Agencies	<1	4	55	<1	37	184
United Kingdom	60	–	–	1	18	380
United States	6	–	4	19	48	3,010
Share of Group in Total Aid Receipts [6]	10	4	10	14	45	7,579

Source: DAC Review, 1971. Annex Table 18.

[1] Including some nonconcessional flows.
[2] Members of C.I.A.P. (Inter-American Committee on the Alliance for Progress).
[3] Excluding India and Pakistan. The share of these two (as they then were) countries in 1968–1970 of bilateral aid from France, EEC, United Kingdom, and United States was 1 percent, 3 percent, 23 percent, and 23 percent respectively. Rounding errors explain the discrepancy between the sum of the shares and 100 percent.
[4] Including India and Pakistan.
[5] "–" represents "negligible" or zero.
[6] Including receipts from multilateral agencies.

the period had some bearing on the high positions of Malta, South Vietnam, Laos, Israel, and Singapore, while political factors prevented one small ex-colony—Rhodesia—from receiving any aid at all.

If we assume Latin American countries to have a political link with the United States somewhat similar to that of ex-colonies to their old metropolitan powers and look at data on aid to groups of recipients with common political affinities of this type broken down by donor, we find that the high explanatory powers of this variable are confirmed. The breaking up of the less-developed world into areas of political interest by donors is clearly indicated by Table 2–10, which shows the proportion of the bilateral flows from France, EEC aid agencies, Great Britain, and the United States that go to "political affinity" groups of less-developed countries. These groups of less-developed countries are the Commonwealth (except India and Pakistan, where sheer size and defense considerations are paramount), French overseas territories and departments, other Franc Zone countries in Africa, Latin America, and "others." Defense arrangements could account for much of the distribution of that aid extended by DAC members whose contribution is not explained in this way: about half of the $3,400-million aid flow from all DAC members to countries not in affinity groups (and excluding India and Pakistan) goes to less-developed countries with whom one or more DAC members has a defense agreement. This issue of the distribution of aid brings us, however, to the question of the *motives* of donors in giving aid at all, and this is the subject matter of the next chapter.

III

MOTIVES

FOR GIVING AID

In the last chapter I described the evolution and structure of the aid programs of the rich countries. In this chapter I turn to an analysis of the motives which the governments of rich countries have for maintaining their aid programs. The existence of aid programs implies that a political decision has been taken to transfer, in one way or another, resources from taxpayers in rich countries to various groups of people in poor countries. This chapter is concerned, then, with the question: On what grounds is such a decision taken? The domestic politics of such decision taking is a separate issue and is the subject matter of the next chapter; here I am concerned only with why donor governments think that their countries should maintain aid programs.

Most people in rich countries, if asked why their countries maintain aid programs, would reply that aid is intended to assist the countries of the Third World in their efforts to accelerate their rate of economic and social development. Most politicians would agree that this is the purpose of aid, although many would add that such development was sought as a means of securing some other objective. It is not, however, generally agreed among those engaged in the study of the problems of poor countries that aid can successfully generate accelerated development.

This lack of agreement is partially due to the fact, noted in Chapter 1, that there is no agreement on what constitutes development. Nor is there any agreement on how best to measure progress in economic and social conditions. For example, in a valiant attempt to derive such a measure the United Nation's Secretariat was only able to conclude: "For all its shortcomings, the rate of growth of GDP seems to provide the best available all-round indication of 'success.'" [1] On the other hand, the president of the World Bank, Robert S. McNamara, recently said: "the evidence accumulates that economic growth alone cannot bring about that steady social transformation of a people without which further advances cannot occur. In short, we have to admit that economic growth . . . will not, of itself, be enough to accomplish our development objectives." [2]

In the past, most members of the development profession tended to take the easy way out of the problem of defining development by simply taking it to be synonymous with economic growth. More recently many have become less confident of such an approach and have argued that although growth does not itself measure development it does measure the capacity of a country to develop. The implication is that development requires resources and the more resources there are available, the easier it is to sustain a process of accelerated development, whatever such a process may involve. In both cases growth in income is seen as the target, in the first case as a direct target and in the second as a proxy for some other target. The attraction—and danger—of such approaches is that they allow respectability to be attached to the application of the simple growth models of the economists to the problems of development. Such models are sometimes, confusingly, designated development models in order to distinguish them from the highly abstract growth models of theoretical economists.

---

[1] *The Measurement of Development Effort* (New York: United Nations, 1971), page 12.

[2] Robert S. McNamara, *Address to the Board of Governors* (Copenhagen: IBRD, 1970), page 21.

Growth and Development: The Apparent Purpose of Aid

Supporters of aid programs frequently bolster their arguments by referring to abstract theoretical models of the economic process in poor countries. The attraction of development models (two examples of which are discussed below, in Chapters 5 and 8) is that they allocate well-defined—and crucial—roles to aid. Typical models hold that economic growth is constrained primarily by inadequate investment. In some models this results because the population of the country does not or cannot save enough of its income to pay for the investment. In others, savings may be adequate; but they cannot be converted into investment as the necessary resources have to be imported, and there is not enough foreign exchange available. In such situations aid can add either to the level of savings the economy can sustain or to the supply of foreign exchange available to savers to use for buying imported investment goods.

Such simplistic models are deficient on two counts—technically and in a public relations sense. They are technically deficient in that they oversimplify the growth process to a level of absurdity. They are deficient in the public relations sense in that unless increased flows of income can be shown to be closely linked to aid flows, critics of aid can argue that aid has not been successful.

Growth is not simply a function of inputs of capital (investable resources), and most notions of development are even less so. Growth depends also on such things as improvements in basic levels of educational attainment, increased supplies of workers with specific skills, and institutional reforms. Development requires also that as growth takes place a given set of social criteria is fulfilled. If there is agreement between donor and recipient government on what these other inputs and social criteria are, it is possible that the donor government can insist that the recipient government take them into account when formulating its economic policies. Even if the donor government insists on such a package deal and even if the recipient government agrees to it, success in terms of accelerated growth and development may not result. The provision of aid does not *guarantee* anything; it can only open up certain limited possibilities.

For one, agreements between donor and recipient may be based on a misunderstanding of the nature of the economic system in the recipient country; the economy simply may not respond to the policies in the way expected. Second, even though politicians and administrators in the recipient country may commit themselves to the policy package in good faith (and some may not), they may not be in a position to implement it. Opposing political and/or economic vested-interest groups may frustrate the government's attempts to implement the agreed on policies. Or the government may find that it has incorrectly estimated the willingness of the people as a whole to have such policies imposed and find itself constrained by the prospects of electoral defeat or even revolution. Third, as already hinted, some recipient governments may have no intention of making anything more than a token attempt to implement the agreed on policies. And fourth, any of a host of stochastic factors—a sudden slump in export earnings, a break in the weather cycle, a major natural disaster, or an unrelated political upheaval—may affect the economy and destroy or distort the potential effectiveness of the policies. 1778079

In the presence of any of the possibilities listed in the last paragraph, the strong link between aid and growth or development which is implied in the popular development models is broken. Such is the tenacity of fixed ideas, however, that aid programs continue to be justified with arguments that development requires economic growth, which in turn requires inputs of goods and services (including knowledge), which are only obtainable by importing them from the rich countries. Such arguments are derived from the popular development models and are used, in reverse, to establish policy prescriptions. It is frequently argued, for example, that aid allows poor countries to increase imports from rich countries, which allows them to raise their rate of economic growth, which in turn supports an accelerated rate of development.

These theoretically based policy prescriptions have tended to become accepted as statements of fact. There are many examples of this tendency. For one, when it presented to Congress the International Development and Humanitarian Assistance Bill of 1971, the U.S. Agency for International Development wrote:

> Development aid is provided to assist the economic and social development of less developed countries i.e. increase their economic growth and distribute available goods and services more widely. . . . Development aid is meant to support economic and social change —to increase agricultural and industrial production, to educate and train people, to help prevent population growth from outrunning economic growth, to build lasting institutions, to reduce economic disparities and promote wider distribution of the benefits of economic progress.[3]

Similarly, the president of the World Bank, Robert S. McNamara, in the 1970 *Address to the Board of Governors* said:

> Over the last decade the developing nations have achieved the historically unprecedented rate of growth of 5 percent a year. This has been made possible in part by a reasonably sustained level of assistance. . . . Growth is a necessary but not a sufficient cause of successful modernization. We must secure a 6 percent growth rate. We must deploy the resources necessary for it. But we must do more. We must ensure that in such critical fields as population planning, rural renewal, fuller employment, and decent urbanism, positive policies support and hasten the social transformation without which economic growth itself becomes obstructed and its results impaired.[4]

And as a third example, one of the most quoted builders of

[3] International Development and Humanitarian Assistance Act of 1971. Presentation to the Congress (by the Agency for International Development of the State Department) of the Proposed FY 1972 Program (Washington, D.C.: Published Government Report, 1971).

[4] McNamara, *Address to the Board of Governors,* page 21.

development models—Professor Hollis B. Chenery—has written: "One of the principal means for poor countries to accelerate their development is by using external resources to supply additional imports and to finance a higher level of investment." [5]

The danger with such statements is that they fix in peoples' minds the notion that aid is positively and always associated with economic growth and social change. The qualifications in the statements tend to be underplayed and ignored. Aid has consequently been oversold. This overselling of aid has not necessarily been a conscious intention of those responsible for it. Many of the relevant administrators who have to "sell" their programs to politicians, and many politicians who have to "sell" them to their constituents, derive their views from their experiences of the Marshall Aid scheme. After World War II the European countries had the necessary social structure and economic and institutional infrastructures needed to sustain economic and social progress. All that was missing was capital; and this was provided in the Marshall Aid Plan, with the result that Western Europe was able to achieve considerable economic and social progress quite rapidly. The models and attitudes developed during the Marshall Plan years were later transferred to the problems of the LDCs, but such a transfer was illegitimate.

One commentator has put it in the following terms:

> In the less-developed countries there is no such simple path to progress as that which faced Western Europe in the years of the Marshall Plan. While simple theoretical models have been developed in which the bottleneck to progress turns out to be, depending on the circumstances, either a shortage of domestic resources (a "savings gap") or a shortage of imported goods (a "foreign exchange gap"), there are at most only a few countries and periods to which such models can be applied in practice. In general, and as is well known, the modernization of backward economies is an enormously complex, difficult and time-consuming process. Barriers to growth abound: social and political elites unreceptive to change, gross deficiences of the technical skills and

[5] H. B. Chenery and A. MacEwan, "Optimal Patterns of Growth and Aid: The Case of Pakistan," *The Pakistan Development Review* (Summer 1966), page 209.

capacities required by modernization, markets that are poorly organized and whose proper functioning is further impaired by ill-conceived public policies, systems of fiscal and foreign-trade policy that in their present state are if anything impediments to rather than promoters of modernization—these constitute only a partial listing. Without belabouring the point, I would suggest that most serious participants in and observers of our history of foreign aid would agree that we have not found to date, and cannot reasonably expect to find in the future the same kind of touchstone to promoting the growth of the less-developed countries as was represented by the provision of physical resources to Western Europe under the Marshall Plan.[6]

The exposure of overoptimistic claims concerning the link between aid and growth and development to critical analysis, and the frequent failure of reality to conform with the predictions of the models and politicians, leads people who believe that high growth rates indicate that development is taking place to the conclusion that aid is more or less useless. Critics of aid go further than this. It has been argued, for example:

> It would be naive to assume that the major objective of foreign assistance is economic development, that either directly or indirectly through political and social change the purpose of foreign aid is to raise the level of material well-being in the receiving country. . . . But we believe that there are other reasons for which aid is given, and by which the donor countries judge its effectiveness. . . . [We believe] that economic aid from the powerful to the powerless, from the metropole to the satellites, is an instrument of power politics. How much a country lends to another country will not be determined by its need, or its potential, or its past economic performance, good or bad, or its virtue, but by the benefit it yields in terms of political support.[7]

But this argument is naive too.

Different people can support the same program for different reasons. Many people professionally or politically involved in

[6] From A. C. Harberger, "Issues Concerning Capital Assistance to Less-Developed Countries," *Economic Development and Cultural Change* (July 1972).

[7] K. B. Griffin and J. L. Enos, "Foreign Assistance: Objectives and Consequences," *Economic Development and Cultural Change* (April 1970), pages 314, 315.

aid programs do believe that aid is and should be provided simply to enable poor countries to develop more quickly, and obviously they believe that aid *can* enable them to do so. Whatever the basis for their beliefs, they become disillusioned with aid when the indicators of development they use do not show positive gains. The problem is, at least partially, one of measurement; for even when accepted indicators of development show negative results, aid may be supporting real and important development. Let us take an extreme example, to make this simple but crucial point, that of a predominantly agricultural country in which most income and most exports are derived from the agricultural sector. A combination of poor weather and a slump in export markets would normally result in a low or negative growth rate over such a period. Let us further assume that aid is being used to support long-term projects in education, road building, and low-cost housing and that some aid finance can be quickly diverted to financing imports of food to forestall the danger of hunger or starvation in the countryside and/or riots in the towns. These aid-financed ventures and the essential consumption support would have little impact on short-run growth figures. *But* as the average level of educational attainment, of access to communication and of mobility of the rural population, the quality of the housing of the poor, and the measures to prevent hunger and starvation are improved, few would deny that development is taking place.

Aid may, then, contribute significantly to the economic growth of some less-developed countries, and it may also contribute to their socioeconomic development. It has, however, been argued above that the links claimed to exist between aid and these objectives are not clear-cut and that consequently it is dangerous to justify aid programs entirely in terms of such objectives. Taxpayers in donor countries have, however, been led to believe that such links exist. On the one hand, this means that while they are taxed to provide aid, they expect to see evidence of growth or development taking place. Their continued support of aid programs will depend on the existence of such evidence.

On the other hand, it raises a further question: Why do taxpayers in donor countries consider it in their interest to forego income in order to accelerate the socioeconomic well-being of the inhabitants of the Third World? Or, to put it another way: How do politicians and aid officials of donor countries convince their taxpayers that such a sacrifice is worthwhile?

Actual Purposes for Giving Aid: The U.S. View

Taxpayers in rich countries are told by their governments that it is necessary for them to pay increased taxes in order to provide aid to poor countries. Much of this aid, they are told, is to enable poor countries to attain higher levels of economic and social well-being, this being (directly or indirectly) in the interest of the donor countries. The debate over whether or not aid *can* achieve its objectives—be they explicit or implicit—is irrelevant in this context. Aid, for the present at least, continues to flow from rich countries to poor countries; and while vigorous argument goes on about how best to transfer such resources, it is obvious that the policymakers in the rich countries are convinced that it is in their national interest to maintain such flows. Whether or not past aid has or has not stimulated growth or the "right sort" of development, it can always be argued that on the basis of past experience *future* aid will be used more effectively. Thus politicians in rich countries believe that aid can serve their national interests. What are those interests?

In his September 15, 1970, statement to Congress on the U.S. aid program, President Nixon said, "There are three *interrelated* purposes that the United States should pursue through our foreign assistance program: promoting our national security by supporting the security of other nations; providing humanitarian relief; and furthering the long-run economic and social development of the lower income countries." [8] President Nixon in justifying military assistance programs for "friends and allies" argued:

[8] This and the following quotations are from President Nixon's statement as reported in *Front Lines*, vol. 8, no. 24 (Washington, D.C.: AID Publication, September 24, 1970), pages 3–6. The emphasis is mine throughout.

The *national security objectives of the United States* cannot be pursued solely through defense of our territory. They require a successful effort by other countries around the world, *including a number of low income countries,* to mobilize manpower and resources to defend themselves. They require, in some cases, military bases abroad, to give us the necessary ability to defend ourselves and to deter aggression. They sometimes require our *financial support of friendly countries* in exceptional situations.

Concerning the second, humanitarian, purpose of United States aid, President Nixon stated, simply, "The humanitarian concerns of the American people have traditionally led us to provide assistance to foreign countries for relief from natural disasters, to help with child care and maternal welfare, and to respond to needs of international refugees and migrants." And of the third purpose he said—and I quote at length—

Both security and humanitarian assistance serve our basic *national* goal: the creation of a peaceful world. *This* interest is also served, in a fundamental and lasting sense, by the third purpose of our foreign assistance: the building of self-reliant and productive societies in the lower income countries. Because these countries contain two-thirds of the world's population the direction which the development of their societies takes will profoundly affect the world in which *we* live. *We must respond to the needs of these countries if our own country and its values are to remain secure.*

It is outside the scope of this book and of the competence of the author to assess the criteria which governments see as determining the need for and size of their military and humanitarian assistance programs. It is worthwhile noting, however, that as far as development assistance is concerned, President Nixon said in his statement, ". . . the lower income countries have made impressive progress. . . . *The magnitude of their achievement is indicated by the fact that the lower income countries taken together have exceeded the economic growth targets of the first United Nations Development Decade.*" This quotation should be read in conjunction with part of the conclusion to the President's statement, that is:

The U.S. role in international development assistance reflects the vision we have of ourselves as a society and our hope for a peaceful world. Our interest in long-term development must be viewed in the context of *its contribution to our own security*. Economic development will not by itself guarantee the political stability which all countries seek, certainly not in the short run, *but political stability is unlikely to occur without sound economic development*.

It is clear, then, that the U.S. Administration sees the contribution aid makes to the economic and social progress of poor countries as furthering U.S. interests in promoting world political conditions which enhance its own security. The military assistance program can, along with the development assistance program, be viewed as an instrument of U.S. foreign policy. Thus the tax dollar of the U.S. taxpayer which supports those programs does not go unrequited—the *quid pro quo* is his own and his family's security.

Thus, the real test of the effectiveness of an aid dollar, from the point of view of the United States, is how much security it buys for the United States. The crucial nature of this test becomes evident when we consider what are sometimes claimed as proximate, or subsidiary, objectives. It is inconceivable at the present time that the United States would finance any form of economic development in China or Cuba. Equally, there is no doubt that any request from Albania for support for child care and maternity centers would receive scant attention. Any economic or social development which might have resulted from such aid would be regarded as self-defeating in the sense of contributing to a *reduction* in the security of the United States. Meanwhile, U.S. aid is extended to dictators and oligarchs who have little concern with the economic and social well-being of the poorer people in their countries.

There was a reason in choosing extreme examples in the last paragraph. It was to illustrate the point that if the purpose of aid is to enhance the sense of national security felt by those in charge of foreign policy, then it is not possible to measure unequivocally the efficiency of aid. All that the references to security and peace in President Nixon's statement imply is that foreign policymakers in the United States sometimes see a potential threat to U.S. security deriving from a threat to political stability in a country they regard as playing an important part in the overall defense of the United States. In such cases they will advocate the extension of assistance to the government of that country. If the threat seen to the stability of the country is aggressive in nature, from without or within the frontiers of the country, the aid is likely to be basically or predominately military in nature. If the threat is seen to derive from the dissatisfaction of the population of the country due to discontent with economic and social conditions, then the assistance will be economic, perhaps with social strings attached. Either form of aid will be given only if the foreign policymakers in the United States believe that the regime being supported can reduce or minimize the threat to the security of U.S. interests. Clearly, there is no way in which the strength and validity of such beliefs can be accurately measured.

Security

President Nixon's policy toward aid, as reflected in the message to Congress quoted above, is derived from an assumed causality between aid, economic and social progress, political stability, and the security of U.S. interests. Apart from the problem of defining what such terms mean, there are reasons to doubt that this assumed chain of causality actually exists. I have already indicated doubts about the theories that aid leads to economic growth and that economic growth leads to social progress. The chairman of the OECD Development Assistance Committee wrote in his report for 1971: "The benefits of 5 percent growth (of the total GNP of the Third World) since 1960 have often been enjoyed primarily by a limited number of people, leaving the majority of the populations of most developing countries, i.e. the subsistence farmers, farm labourers, urban unemployed, etc., no better off." [9] President Nixon in his statement recognized that, in the short run, socioeconomic progress which might result from aid need not produce political stability. Indeed, he recognized that tensions could be created between groups as a result of rapid socioeconomic development. He went on, however, to claim that *in the long run*, socioeconomic progress was a prerequisite for political stability. There is no evidence, in history or theory, to support this belief.

Political stability in a country depends for its existence on the satisfaction of its people with their lot. The history of civilization does not lend credence to the belief that improvement in social and economic conditions leads to such satisfaction nor, therefore, to political stability. Indeed many changes in the social and economic conditions of a people generally accepted as being "progressive" directly lead to its dissatisfaction, which is then translated into political instability. Innovations such as radio, television, airplanes, and even improved seeds and educational reform have been identified by social scientists as creating an "horizon of rising expectations," which when frustrated lead to political tensions.

> This wave of innovation has served to remind us that there is no simple causal link between economic development and "political stability," i.e. evolutionary as opposed to revolutionary change. What does seem clear is that economic growth will not be the basis for the orderly progress of any society unless it is sufficiently rapid and broadly based materially to benefit a wide cross-section of that society. To favour the best-placed landowners does not contribute to stability. Nor is it helpful to free men from the drudgery of manual farm labour only to provide them with no alternative livelihood. A man without work in a congested city may pose a far bigger political problem than one without food in a village.[10]

[9] Organization for Economic Cooperation and Development. *Development Assistance: Efforts and Policies of the Members of the Development Assistance Committee. 1971 Review*, page 12. Paris, 1971.

[10] Neville Brown, "Underdevelopment as a Threat to World Peace," *International Affairs* (April 1971), page 337.

If we can throw doubt on the hypothesized links between aid, socioeconomic progress, and political stability, we can regard the final link—between political stability and the apparently ultimate objective of aid, the security of donor interests—as no more than wishful thinking. The first question we ask in connection with this final link is: Security of what? We can identify three basic concepts of security which rich countries attempt to attain through their aid programs: military (or territorial) security, economic (or commercial) security, and political security. It can be argued that those in control of the aid programs of donor countries will provide aid to countries which they believe to be actual or potential threats to the military, economic, or political interests of their own countries or which they believe could assist the donor country in defending such interests. This argument would appear to be supported by the data on the distribution of aid.

Few politicians in donor countries worry about the prospect of a direct attack on their territories by less-developed countries. Their military interests in less-developed countries are twofold: first they seek to maintain peace among poor countries so that they will not be drawn into a third world war; and second they seek to contain the influence of "enemy" powers or hostile ideologies by maintaining bases or strong allies in poor countries. Much U.S. and some European aid can be attributed to such motives. Aid recipients such as Spain, Turkey, Malta, South Korea, Laos, South Vietnam, Greece, and Israel (not all of which would be classified as poor countries) owe their inclusion in the aid programs simply to the strategic position they are believed to hold by military strategists and politicians in rich countries. In such cases aid is provided either as "rent" for military bases maintained in the countries by the donors or to gain the allegiance of those in control of the recipients' armed forces. The actual use made of the (economic) aid is irrelevant to the donor as long as these objectives are secured, although attempts may be made by the donors to insure that some, at least, is used for generally recognized "development" purposes, in order to widen political support for the program among donor politicians and taxpayers.

Over the years the rich countries have become increasingly dependent on the poor countries for supplies of some raw materials and for markets for their own products. In addition, firms in rich countries have invested heavily in poor countries in order to take advantage of their resources and markets. The rich countries, therefore, see an interest in maintaining the security of such investments, sources of supply, and markets. Aid is consciously used to serve such interests. Such is the identification of commercial self-interest with aid programs in rich countries, that most donors include private investment by their national firms in their statistics on aid. No one in the United States would consider investment by ITT in France to be American aid to France, but such investment in a poor country is often counted in the aid total. No one in the United States would consider providing official aid to France in order to gain access for U.S. investors to that market, but poor countries are frequently threatened by the U.S. government with a suspension of aid if they consider taking over, in one way or another, U.S.-owned firms. The United States and Great Britain have, in fact, brought pressure to bear on the World Bank Group in attempts to get that institution to cease providing aid to countries which have nationalized property belonging to their nationals, without providing compensation considered adequate by the U.S. and British governments.

While the motive of military security probably predominates in the minds of those who control and support the U.S. aid program, in the cases of Great Britain, Japan, Germany, Australia, and the European Communities as an institution the economic motive is probably the most important determinant of aid levels and distribution. While recognition is generally given to the concept of the responsibility of rich countries to assist poor countries in their efforts to develop, official statements on aid in these countries tend to stress the economic advantage accruing to the donor. Thus a Select Committee of the House of Commons reported:

Britain is an aid donor not only because of her concern for the welfare of the peoples of the developing world but also for reasons of mutual advantage. . . . The prosperity of Britain is closely bound up with that of the developing world, which in turn is bound up with the international aid effort. . . . Commercial considerations alone would suffice to justify participation in the aid effort, both bilaterally and through international agencies.[11]

In the case of Great Britain, although the existence and size of the aid program may be primarily justified in terms of economic self-interest, the distribution of the aid is affected by the nation's imperial past. Eighty-three percent of official British bilateral aid over the period 1968 to 1970 went to Commonwealth countries. This was, however, somewhat affected by the presence of India and (the then) Pakistan in the Commonwealth, these two areas of chronic and extensive poverty receiving 23 percent of total official British bilateral aid over the period. Although little British aid goes to ex-Commonwealth Burma, and Tanzania temporarily ceased receiving aid when it broke off diplomatic relations with Great Britain, it is probable that the existence and size of the British aid effort is not affected by its membership in the Commonwealth. In the case of France, however, it is probably true to say that its aid effort is primarily a function of its desire to maintain cultural, political, and economic ties with its ex-colonies and remaining imperial outposts—the overseas territories and departments. This brings us to the third interest for which donors seek security: political interests.

Political motives for giving aid are many and diverse, and any commentator attempting to argue that a donor is extending aid because it feels a need to safeguard its political interests is likely to be accused of, among other things, bias. If I say that the fundamental reason why the French maintain a bilateral aid program is their desire to defend the French language, I can support my case by pointing out that President Pompidou used

[11] From paragraphs 10 and 11 of the *Report from the Select Committee on Overseas Aid*. House of Commons, Session 1970–1971. (London: Her Majesty's Stationery Office, March 1971).

those very words to defend the continuance of French bilateral aid.[12] If I go on to say that the reason the French wish to defend the French language is because they wish to defend their position as a world power and hope to buy this position by keeping their colonies and ex-colonies dependent on them for aid, I am simply stating an opinion. If I go on to justify this opinion by pointing out that France has the lowest ratio of multilateral to bilateral aid of the major donors, that 23 percent of French bilateral aid goes to her overseas territories and departments, that another 60 percent goes to her ex-colonies, and that when Guinea chose to leave the Franc Zone, French aid to that country ceased abruptly, I can be accused of inconsistency. Similarly, I cannot provide conclusive proof of my belief that the smaller donors— the Nordic countries, Austria, Belgium, the Netherlands, and Italy—maintain aid programs only because the other Western countries have such programs, and they feel they must, too, in order to be seen to be sharing the burden. I would argue that they accept this burden because they wish to maintain friendly relations with the richer donors, but I cannot prove this, as the only test would be to see what they did if the richer donors stopped providing aid. I do make these statements, though, as I believe them to be true and to be consistent with such evidence as is available: this is, as I explained in Chapter 1, *my* political economy of aid.

Conclusion

This chapter has been addressed to the question: Why do rich countries maintain aid programs? Most donor governments put out platitudinous official statements to the effect that they provide aid to poor countries because they recognize a responsibility to help those countries improve the welfare of their citizens. Such statements are, however, part of the rhetoric of aid and beg the further question: Why do politicians in donor countries, and

[12] In a speech to the Assemblée Nationale, June 10, 1964. See the *Journal Official*, p. 1785.

their voters, feel it a worthwhile use of their tax revenues and payments to provide such assistance to poor countries? They would not do so if they believed that they were acting *against* their own interests. In this chapter I have, in effect, argued that the real motives for providing aid, that is, the arguments that politicians use to convince themselves and their voters, are fear and greed. I have argued that the eventualities which donors seek to insure against include involvement in war, encirclement by hostile powers, disruption of sources of supply and access to markets, and loss of face or stature in world forums. I have argued also that aid is provided out of a desire to guarantee increased supplies of food and raw materials and to guarantee rights of exploration of resources and market exploitation. I have suggested that aid may not in fact lead to (or be intended to lead to) social or economic development, or political stability in poor countries, or security of the military, economic, and political interests of donor countries.

Many people in donor countries have doubts about the arguments and motives of the pro-aid lobbies and question the effectiveness of aid as a means of serving donor interests. While I have doubts about the nature and strength of the assumed causality between aid, development, political stability, and security, others have categorical views. The juxtaposition of the views of these antiaid lobbies and those of the pro-aid lobbies in donor countries constitutes the domestic politics of aid. This is the subject matter of the next chapter.

IV

THE DOMESTIC
POLITICS OF AID

In previous chapters the not very startling assumption was made that on the whole taxpayers prefer their tax bills to be as low as possible. Most people, however, accept that governments must pay for some of their expenditures by raising taxes. Much political discussion revolves around the question of what expenditures governments should undertake. Unless governments are authoritarian, they are forced at some stage to explain to their electorate the necessity of their paying taxes to cover proposed expenditures. Whenever a democratic government proposes to the electorate, or its elected representatives, that it be taxed in order to finance particular government policies, there are always political parties, lobbies, interest groups, and individuals on hand ready to support or criticize the government's proposals. It is within this schema that the domestic politics of aid take place.

In Chapter 3, concerned as it was with the motives for giving aid, the emphasis was placed on pro-aid arguments. In this chapter such arguments are briefly reviewed from the taxpayer's standpoint, while emphasis is given to arguments presented to him favoring the abolition or substantial reduction of aid. Given the assumption that people on the whole prefer not to pay taxes, I discuss the effects of the pro and anti arguments on public

50

opinion, and, in turn, the effects of public opinion on government aid policy. The chapter goes on to discuss the "rhetoric" of aid—that is, the way in which the same government policy is justified to different groups in completely different terms. As aid cannot in fact be "all things to all men" some people will, on the basis of the rhetoric, give their support to an aid program only to discover later that it achieves much less than they were led to believe it would. Such disillusionment, which has increased significantly in recent years, turns sections of public opinion against aid, with an eventual impact on policy formulation. Later in this chapter I show how this process has unfolded in the United States in recent years, and how widespread disenchantment with aid affected the progress of aid legislation through Congress in 1971.

The Voters' Viewpoint

In free societies whenever a felt need for action is shared by a number of people, some kind of institution, commercial or public service, will be created to satisfy that need. In all countries at all times there have been minorities who have felt a need to help people they consider to be worse off than themselves. Over the years many thousands of charitable institutions have been created to enable such minorities to aid the poor in various ways. These institutions have been for the most part free from political controversy. They have, in fact, tended consciously to steer clear of political involvement and have generally concentrated on providing assistance for individuals within their own country. (Exceptions to this are most frequently found in countries with a recent imperial past, where a missionary zeal for "unfortunate" people overseas has traditionally been inculcated in the young.) Occasionally, however, where the charitable institution gains widespread or vocal support among its electorate, a government may feel compelled to translate the felt need of the institution into government policy and attempt to remove the cause of the suffering in question or to provide compensation for it. Thus, in recent history many governments have taken over from charitable institutions their self-imposed responsibility for orphans, sick or disabled people, and the unemployed. Just as there were, and are, critics of governments' attempts to assist such people, so many people in rich countries now criticize their governments for their having assumed a responsibility to assist the inhabitants of poor countries and their having decided to pay for such assistance out of tax revenues.

Many, perhaps most, people are so self-interested that they will not admit the possibility that paying over some part of their income to the government in taxes in order to enable it to assist other people in the improvement of their lot may increase the total amount of welfare being enjoyed by the world's population. Some even insist that alleviating a person's poverty is not in the poor person's interest, as it removes the incentive he has to attempt to improve his own lot and turns him into a social parasite. Where the poor people he is being asked to pay taxes to assist are foreigners, the taxpayer may argue that their welfare is not his country's responsibility but that of their own government. This position is frequently strengthened when rich citizens of the poor country visit the taxpayer's home country or when the governments of poor countries engage in seemingly (or certainly) wasteful expenditures. Such nationalistic tendencies are further intensified if there is much poverty and social inequality in the taxpayer's own country. We can label the above reasons as being those which politically conservative groups may use to support their case for their not being taxed to provide aid funds. We can add to the list some arguments against aid which have been put forward by groups usually regarded as politically liberal or radical.

Many of the liberal and radical arguments against aid derive from the belief that the aid process necessarily involves donors in the domestic affairs of recipient countries. Radicals argue that such involvement is never desirable, while liberals more often feel that involvement may result in the maintenance in power of reactionary or corrupt governments in the recipient countries or in longer term economic, social, or military commitments which they would consider undesirable. More recently, radical leaders of some minority groups in donor countries—for example, blacks in the United States—have been vocal in their opposition to their countries' aid programs, as they feel a stronger case can be made for allocating such government expenditures to programs for improving the welfare of their own particular group. Recently, too, radical youth movements in donor countries have argued that, as they consider their own governments to be corrupt or inept, manipulated by industrial, commercial, and military interests, then they must conclude that any involvement with poor countries resulting from aid flows must be exploitative in nature and, therefore, must worsen the situation. This conviction is strengthened when private enterprises and individuals in donor countries are seen to reap vast corporate and personal incomes from aid.[1]

The last few paragraphs have indicated reasons why some groups in donor countries may oppose the provision of any aid at all to poor countries. There may be others who accept in general that their governments should operate tax-financed aid programs but feel, at any period in time, that the total flow involved is too large (or too small). Other groups who favor aid in general may oppose the form of their own government's program; they may not agree with their government's choice of recipients or method of distribution. For example, some Americans are opposed to their government's provision of aid to South Vietnam and some oppose their government's policy of channeling aid through international agencies. For all these and other similar reasons, at any point in time a government which

---

[1] For examples of those attitudes and arguments see the following: Africa Research Group, *International Dependency in the 1970's* (Cambridge, Mass.: Africa Research Group, 1970); Theodore Geiger, *The Conflicted Relationship: The West and the Transformation of Asia, Africa and Latin America* (New York: McGraw-Hill Book Company, 1967); Dennis Goulet and Michael Hudson, *The Myth of Aid: The Hidden Agenda of the Development Reports* (New York: IDOC North America and Orbis Books, 1971); and The Haslemere Group, *The Haslemere Declaration* (London: The Haslemere Committee, 1968).

has decided to mount an aid program—for any of the reasons discussed in Chapter 3—will find groups of its electorate (and their representatives) who oppose that decision. It will similarly find groups who support that decision, either because they agree with the purpose the government has in mind or because they have reasons of their own (perhaps because they stand to receive direct financial benefits from the program) for supporting it that are not inconsistent with those of the government.

In the last chapter reasons why governments may wish to maintain aid programs were discussed. In the previous paragraph it was indicated that there are groups of the public in donor countries who support such programs because they agree with the avowed or supposed purposes of the programs, or because their self-interest is served by such programs. Thus, those who believe that the expansion of communist influence and power in the world should be suppressed and thwarted and who also believe that aid can help suppress and thwart this expansion are in favor of aid programs. Many people in the rich countries, especially in the United States, supported their country's aid programs for this reason in the early years of the Cold War. Other people, individually or collectively through organizations to which they belong, support their country's aid programs because they feel a moral obligation to help their less fortunate fellow human beings in poor countries. Conspicuous in this "lobby" are religious organizations throughout the rich part of the world; other, less obvious, groups support aid programs on moral grounds—an example in the United States is the League of Women Voters.

Groups who support aid programs out of self-interest (or because they seek to further the interests of identifiable groups in the poorer countries) are more likely to favor specific forms of aid. Manufacturers favor aid if it involves increased sales of (and possibly higher prices for) their products; farmers in the United States are vociferous supporters of aid-financed sales of their surplus produce under the Public Law 480, "Food for Peace" program. Jewish groups in the United States support aid for Israel. Politicians favor increased aid if it involves increased business, profits, and employment for the areas they represent. (On the other hand, politicians generally oppose aid if it is likely to put business, profits, and employment in those areas in jeopardy). Other well-identified sources of support for aid programs in rich countries are those manufacturers, financial and banking concerns, and other business houses who have large investments in poor countries. Their support for aid derives from a belief that aid can effectively add to the security and/or profitability of their investments.

The Effectiveness of Public Opinion

There is no reason why the aid program a government decides to mount should accurately reflect the views of the majority of its electorate toward aid. Governments do not rise or fall as a result of their policies toward aid. Indeed, very few voters allocate their vote according to a political party's, or candidate's, views on aid. Aid policies pale into political insignificance when contrasted in most voters' minds with other issues, and, consequently, aid plans do not figure prominently (if they are included at all) in election manifestoes. Still less do incumbent governments feel any strong need to trim the sails of their aid policies to match the wind of electoral opinion (although they may and do from time to time counter criticism of their aid policies by referring to electoral opinion). As the resources involved are only a small part of total government expenditure and as electoral opinion is very much more sensitive to other aspects of government policy, governments feel free (within broad limits) to mount whatever aid program appeals to them most. In a fundamental sense governments are in a position to act as leaders in the field of aid policy.

Donor governments have in general, however, failed to make an expansion of their countries' aid programs an important feature of their policy. This failure to provide a strong political lead in support of aid is perhaps best exemplified by the fact

that whenever a donor government runs into economic difficulties, at home or abroad, the aid budget is most often one of the
first items of government expenditure to be cut. For example,
when President Nixon introduced his "New Economic Policy"
(in August 1971) in response to what he and his advisers felt
was a balance of payments crisis, one of the major components
of that policy package was a 10 percent cut in foreign aid.

A basic problem in the politics of aid is that while donor governments as such have tended to underplay and overlook aid
questions, many individual politicians are only too willing to
jump on the permanently running bandwagon of taxpayers'
antipathy to taxes. While advocacy of cuts in most items of
public expenditure in most donor countries would run up
against vociferous and powerful resistance from domestic interest groups, cuts in aid can be advocated relatively safely; for
by its very nature, fewer nationals are dependent on it for a
livelihood. Such resistance as there is to advocacy of cuts in aid
can be, and frequently is, dismissed by the politician as the irrelevant criticism of "long-haired intellectuals" and "do-gooders"
only too willing to spend other peoples' tax money.

Voters in donor countries are frequently ignorant of the size,
purpose, and nature of the aid programs their tax money supports. Most believe that the programs are larger than they are,
that aid is provided entirely in the form of outright grants, and
that aid funds are usually corruptly embezzled by politicians
in recipient countries. For example, in an opinion poll taken in
England in 1970, only 21 percent of those surveyed were in favor
of an increase in aid. (Thirty-seven percent favored a reduction
in the level of aid and the remaining 42 percent favored keeping aid the same or did not know.) Yet when the same people
were asked if they thought that the U.K. government should
allocate 2½ percent of its total budget to aid, 56 percent of them
said yes. Such an allocation of government income to aid would
have involved more than doubling the size of the actual U.K.
aid program. In the United States a survey of people with college educations found that two-thirds of them believe that the

U.S. aid program is running at a level more than five times its actual size.[2] This situation allows politicians to play on public ignorance for their own ends and allows them to gain favor among their constituents with speeches about the need to reduce the "flow of tax money down the aid drain."

The paradox of the politics of aid is, then, that while a politician may seek favor among his constituents by calling for cuts in aid, he need not take such a stance at the parliamentary or national level. This is so because, as I have argued above, of the many political issues facing an electorate at any one time the question of aid is seldom if ever a vote-swaying issue. Thus, while a politician *may* take a parliamentary or national stand against aid (supporting his argument by referring to the hostile opinion among his constituents which he himself did so much to create), it is possible for him to speak against aid in his constituency, not to refer to it at all in his parliamentary work, and to come out, as many do, in favor of it in international circles, without jeopardizing his political career. This willingness to make speeches in favor of aid (for chosen audiences) without backing them up with a willingness to initiate or press for supporting legislative action has led to what may be called the "rhetoric of aid."

The Rhetoric of Aid

In recent years many donor governments and some of their political leaders have contributed to what I have called the rhetoric of aid. This rhetoric—extolling the virtues of aid in general and drawing attention to what the rhetoricians regard as the virtues of their own government's aid program—is primarily designed for international consumption, although it also calms the fears of domestic pro-aid lobbies. The concern for international opinion is a function of the growing awareness in the international community, especially in United Nations for-

[2] "Public Opinion," *Internationalist* (November 1971), page 18. Unsigned article.

ums, of the extent and urgency of economic and social problems faced by the poor countries of the Third World. This growing awareness reflects the fact that as colonies have become sovereign nations with membership in international forums, there have been many more voices to draw attention to the problem. To the extent, then, that the rich countries have felt it necessary to maintain friendly relations with the new countries, and to the extent that they have believed that aid could insure such friendship, the governments of rich countries and their representatives have felt it necessary to be seen to be contributing to the total flow of aid. Moreover, being politicians, they have felt it necessary to make "promises" of even more aid in the future and to make their individual contributions to existing flows seem as generous as possible. We saw in Chapter 2 how donor governments can present data on their aid programs to make them appear to be more generous than they, in fact, are. (This exaggerated generosity is partly aimed at other donors in order to persuade them to increase their contribution to the total aid flow.)

The Aid Backlash

When the rhetoric of aid is confronted with the facts of aid, when promises do not materialize and the supposed generosity appears more like parsimony, then, hardly surprisingly, the expected friendship frequently does not manifest itself or appears muted. The intelligent domestic voter, in observing this scene, sees only three conflicting phenomena. He is first of all aware of the failure of his politicians to stress the need for aid programs when seeking his vote; they may even have condemned aid outright. Secondly, he sees the leaders of his government making grandiloquent speeches at the United Nations in which they stress how large and meaningful their aid program is—and how much larger and more meaningful it will soon be. If the voter questions his representative about this apparently ambivalent position he is likely to hear an apologia derived from the belief that some aid is necessary in order to insure friendly neighbors and a peaceful world. Third, if, as often happens, a recipient of his country's aid acts, or speaks through its representatives to his government, in a way he believes unfriendly, the voter will conclude that the aid program has failed, and he will be moved to form and express opinions which he did not have (or held apathetically) prior to his exposure to the rhetoric.

While the scenario sketched above is not equally accurate for all donors, the existence of a negative feedback from the international politics of aid onto the domestic politics of aid has certainly been present over the last decade or so. Although it is not possible to estimate quantitatively the effect of this feedback, it is certainly true that in many donor countries the electoral apathy has turned into disillusionment. While the taxpayers' votes have not been sought by promises of aid programs, the use of their money has been justified in the face of criticism in terms of ambitious objectives, which have visibly not been achieved —and in the nature of things probably never could have been achieved. For example, although the U.S. aid program expanded rapidly in the early 1960s as part of President Kennedy's much advertised "grand design," the friendship, peace, and economic development in poor countries which U.S. taxpayers were led to expect would result did not materialize. The increasing frequency of armed conflict in several recipients of U.S. aid, the occurrence of U.S. military involvement in some other recipient countries (Dominican Republic and South Vietnam), and a growing hostility toward U.S. "presence" (partly a result of the growth in aid) in many poor countries led to a backlash of opinion against U.S. aid among U.S. taxpayers.

The average taxpayer in donor countries sees his tax money being sent as aid (and most believe that all aid is *given* away) to countries who are drawn most frequently to his attention because of their hostility to, or alienation from, his country or countrymen. From time to time he reads reports in his newspaper of poor countries, which receive aid from his government, signing treaties with countries he regards as enemies. On his television the taxpayer may see representatives of his country being spat at, insulted, kidnapped, or attacked in countries which receive aid from his government: the picture of President Nixon (as Vice-President in the Eisenhower Administration) being spat at and jeered in Argentina and other Latin American countries is still warm in the minds of many U.S. taxpayers. He may see news reports of mobs in poor countries attacking, looting, and burning his country's embassies, other overseas government offices, or business premises and property owned by his fellow citizens. He may come across cases of recipient country governments expropriating, nationalizing, or severely controlling the operation of firms based in his country—perhaps the firm he works for. Even more frequently he will come across evidence of waste, corruption, and incompetence in poor countries. Newspapers in donor countries often carry stories of socially wasteful building or prestige projects and activities in what he has been taught are countries whose inhabitants live in conditions of desperate poverty. He may read stories of individual citizens of Third World countries who have built up vast fortunes, perhaps corruptly, and perhaps even at *his* expense if the aid money provided by his government has been misappropriated.

The phenomena catalogued in the last paragraph (and others of a similar type) do occur frequently and serve to confirm critics of aid in their views, turn doubters into critics, and shake the confidence of some traditional supporters of aid. But perhaps some recent developments have had a more powerful effect on public and political opinion in donor countries. Two developments in particular have raised electors' voices against their national aid programs. The first is the frequency with which poor countries seem to resort to war as a means of settling differences among themselves. Second, and paradoxically, where poor countries have achieved successful development in parts of their economies, some groups in donor countries have reacted violently in response to their successes.

It takes little effort to bring to mind a fairly lengthy list of wars (or conflicts falling short of actual war) which have taken place among less-developed countries over the last two decades. There have been the Israeli-Arab, India-Pakistan, Central American, Indonesia-Malaysia, Vietnamese, and East African conflicts; the civil wars in the Congo, Nigeria, Malaysia, Pakistan, and Algeria; and military repression of armed insurrection in numerous poor countries (e.g. Colombia, Guatemala, Peru, and Uruguay). The taxpayer weighs in his mind the cost of such activity and understandably balances it against the tax revenues his government transfers to the combatants in the form of aid. For instance, in December 1971, the two largest recipients of aid—India and Pakistan—seemed to be preparing to go to war with each other to settle the future of East Pakistan. Donor countries urged restraint on both sides and, as a spokesman for President Nixon, Mr. Ronald Ziegler, put it, "The use of military force in the area would not be understood by people of the United States when the countries involved have such urgent needs." In such situations the taxpayer asks himself: Why should I be taxed in order to provide aid to countries who use up vast resources in fighting with one another?

The second development results from the fact that as recipients develop they are increasingly able to compete economically with donors for markets. Initially they compete in their own home markets, thus reducing donors' export opportunities; more recently some have become competitive in the donors' home markets. Political attention in donor countries has concentrated on the second type of competition as the loss of some export markets has generally been compensated for by the opening up of new opportunities. Where aid helps a recipient to develop its agriculture, so reducing its demand for agricultural imports from donors, the donor will turn its attention to other fields. Thus, increased agricultural income expands demand for imported goods, perhaps in the first instance for agricultural inputs, such as tractors and fertilizers, to further enhance agricultural development. The needs of poor countries are great; once one need is satisfied, attention can be turned to others. But loss of their domestic markets to imports from poor countries seems much more serious to donors. Such competition implies that the industries affected have lost their ability to compete, not only on world markets but also in their own home markets, where they have many advantages, such as lower transport costs and familiarity with trade and distribution channels. In this case the industries affected have no choice other than to cut back production, go out of business, or seek government protection. In most cases they seek government protection.

Donor Response to Growing Competition

Persuasive arguments can be and are advanced in favor of donor governments affording some form of protection to industries faced with serious domestic competition from imports from less-developed countries. Their logic is all derived from political considerations rather than economic ones. The basic problem derives from the fact that less-developed countries have developed competitive export lines in products which have a high labor content for a given unit of output, reflecting the greater abundance (relative to capital) of labor in those countries. Consequently, the greater the value of such imports, the more people (workers) are involved in the threat of loss of income in the donor countries; and workers are voters. As the industries involved, textiles and footwear, for example, tend to be geographically concentrated, the elected political representatives in those areas can find a large and vociferous section of their electorates threatened with loss of income and occupation at one time. The representatives clearly have a strong incentive to put pressure on their governments to provide protection for the interests of their constituents, and they do, with increasing success. The argument is frequently made in such debates that countries who can compete economically with donors should not receive aid which may enhance their ability to compete.

Many people in rich countries see aid in terms of old-fashioned charity—food for the hungry, homes for the homeless, and medicine for the sick. But increasingly aid is being used to provide work for the unemployed, education in modern productive methods and skills, and machinery for the modernization and diversification of industry. In short, the objective of aid donors and recipients is the transformation of the *economies* of the poor countries, rather than the creation of some form of international welfare program. And, given the nature and needs of modern industry, it is inevitable that some industries can be run more efficiently in less-developed countries. These industries (given the small size of domestic markets in poor countries) will naturally look for export opportunities in order to take advantage of their competitive position. It is in the interests of the rich countries that this process be encouraged, for by importing from poor countries the products which they produce more efficiently, the rich countries can reorganize their economies in such a way as to improve the efficiency of their overall operation. But while this economic transformation will benefit a donor country as a whole, in the short run some industries will be net gainers and some net losers. Currently, in the absence of any rational policy in donor countries for adapting their economies to take advantage of the developments in poor countries which their aid has encouraged, governments are protecting the short run net losers from competition and are thus slowing down the process of achieving an expanded and more efficient international distribution of economic activity. This situation, of providing aid for development with one hand and of preventing both sides of the aid process from achieving the full benefits of that development with the other, can be called the "paradox of development." It can only be explained and understood in terms of the domestic political environment in rich countries.

The Paradox of Development

The paradox of development is that when rich countries feel strong enough vis-à-vis poor countries to be able to provide them with aid (whether the objective is security, political or economic), that aid often helps the poorer countries to build up stronger economies and so become more able to challenge the economic hegemony of the rich. It will be many decades before the countries of the Third World can deal with the developed countries as equals. However, as long as developed countries feel a need to maintain friendly relations with them—as allies, as markets, as bases for investment, or as sources of food and raw materials—then they will probably find the "price" of that friendship increasing over time as the poor countries grow in strength—economic, political, and eventually military (as in China). That price will be exacted not only in terms of aid—indeed, as donors see given amounts of aid achieving less, they are only too likely to reduce it further—but also in commercial, financial, political, and diplomatic terms.

The several reasons discussed above why public opinion in donor countries turns against aid also make political leaders reassess the "price" being paid for their foreign aid policy. Some leaders in donor countries feel that in some cases of "unfriendly" acts against them, such as expropriation of donor property, it is essential that all aid should be cut off. Almost all withdrawals of aid have followed acts of recipient governments considered unfriendly by donor governments. Many recipient regimes in poor countries who act in unfriendly or even hostile ways toward their own poor citizens continue, however, to receive aid as long as they maintain friendly relations with donor governments. Where the donor governments feel that a friendly regime is threatened by unfriendly opposition, they may make strenuous efforts, supported with economic and military assistance, to maintain the incumbent government in power, even if it is known to be unpopular with the majority of its citizens and, indeed, even if it is known to be worsening the lot of its own poor. In such cases the rhetoric of aid is stripped bare of its pretences and shown to be nothing more than donor expenditure serving donor ends. It is to such cases that liberal and radical pro-aid groups in donor countries draw attention, with the result that the majority of the donor electorates who do favor aid for humanitarian reasons become disenchanted with the aid activities of their own governments.

The consequence of all this is that aid is increasingly divorced from the needs of the poor people in those less-developed countries to which the rhetoric of aid refers. Antiaid groups and their leaders in donor countries are confirmed in their views by the activities of recipient governments. Political leaders in donor countries who see aid primarily as a tool of foreign policy lose faith in its effectiveness as the costs of achieving policy objectives rise. And pro-aid groups in donor countries become disenchanted when they see their governments attempting to use aid to maintain in power governments in recipient countries who have no concern for their poor. The task of those groups in donor countries who have not lost faith in the possibility of using aid to help the poor is made continually more difficult for all those reasons. As they try to counter the antiaid groups by becoming more vocal in support of aid, they run the risk of being discredited by claiming too much for aid. Many of the arguments developed so far, in general or abstract ways, can perhaps be usefully illustrated by examining the way aid legislation is dealt with in the largest donor country—the United States.

U.S. Aid Legislation

Given the complexity of the U.S. legislative structure covering the U.S. aid program, attention will be primarily directed at U.S. legislation concerning its bilateral development assistance program. To do this an examination will be made of the evolution and progress through the government machine of the International Development and Humanitarian Assistance Act of 1971. Conveniently, 1971 is a useful and an interesting year to take for examining the progress of aid legislation, as for the previous ten years aid legislation consisted solely of consolidating and extending the Foreign Assistance Act of 1961, which embodied President Kennedy's aid policies. In his first message to Congress after his election, President Nixon announced that he was going to undertake a major review of U.S. aid policy and that he would eventually send a bill to Congress proposing a major restructuring of U.S. aid policies. To help him in drawing up "comprehensive recommendations concerning the role of the United States in assistance to less developed countries," he appointed a presidential task force on September 29, 1969. While waiting for the report of the task force, President Nixon (on February 18, 1970) presented a report to Congress entitled "United States Foreign Policy for the 1970s," in which he said that he expected "a new approach to foreign assistance to be one of (the U.S.'s) major foreign policy initiatives in the coming years."

The task force, under the chairmanship of Mr. Rudolph Peterson of the Bank of America, reported to the President on March 4, 1970. In preparing its report:

> the Task Force met with the Cabinet members most concerned with these problems, with the Administrator of the Agency for International Development, and with the heads of other government agencies. It benefited from extensive discussions with their advisers and from excellent papers prepared by their staffs. It had meetings with Members of Congress, business groups, university experts, journalists, and representatives of civic organizations, voluntary agencies, and foundations, around the country. It asked for, and received, carefully considered statements from labor and business and professional committees. It examined in detail the comprehensive report on this subject by the Commission of distinguished international experts headed by former Canadian Prime Minister Lester Pearson. It also studied reports by Governor Nelson Rockefeller, the Perkins Committee, the Committee for Economic Development, the National Planning Association, and other groups. And it commissioned studies on specific subjects from experts in the field.[3]

In other words, for the first time in many years a serious effort was made to take into account the considered opinions of people and groups involved in or interested in aid when drawing up

[3] This and other quotations in the succeeding paragraphs are taken from the *Report of the Peterson Commission,* "U.S. Foreign Assistance in the 1970s: A New Approach" (Washington, D.C.: U.S. Government Printing Office, March 1970), pages iii and 2–4.

legislative plans, though it should be noted that no attempt was made to assess the views of the man-in-the-street.

Bound by its terms of reference to ignore questions bearing on the cost (tax burden) of aid, it was confined to taking account of the opinions of people and organized groups identified as being *committed* to a definite view one way or another on U.S. aid policy. As the largest antiaid group is the American electorate-at-large, which is not organized and is not committed to any one view, the task force necessarily ignored the opinions concerning the U.S. aid program of those ultimately responsible for paying for it. It is, therefore, not surprising that the task force found that, "Many with whom (they) consulted are deeply troubled by particular aspects of U.S. foreign assistance programs and by the apathy and misunderstanding that seem to surround the issues." Nor is it surprising, considering that virtually all the people or groups consulted have a self-imposed or self-interested concern with U.S. foreign policy, that they found, "virtually all (of the people they consulted) believe that the United States has a large stake and serious responsibilities in international development." Taking all this into account, and allowing for the fact that the task force itself was mostly composed of people known to be generally in favor of aid, it is not surprising that it produced a report in favor of aid and presented several arguments justifying that position, reflected in its first conclusion: "The United States has a profound national interest in cooperating with developing countries in their efforts to improve conditions of life in their societies."

Among its other conclusions were the following.[4]

All peoples, rich and poor alike, have common interests in peace, in the eradication of poverty and disease, in a healthful environment, and in higher living standards. It should be a cardinal aim of U.S. foreign policy to help build an equitable political and economic order in which the world's people, their governments, and other institutions can effectively share resources and knowledge.

[4] Only those conclusions relevant to the discussion of the chapter are quoted.

This country should not look for gratitude or votes, or any specific short-term foreign policy gains from our participation in international development. Nor should it expect to influence others to adopt U.S. cultural values or institutions. Neither can it assume that development will necessarily bring political stability. Development implies change—political and social, as well as economic—and such change, for a time, may be disruptive.

What the United States should expect from participation in international development is steady progress toward its long-term goals: the building of self-reliant and healthy societies in developing countries, an expanding world economy from which all will benefit, and improved prospects for world peace.

The United States should keep to a steady course in foreign assistance, providing its fair share of resources to encourage those countries that show a determination to advance. Foreign assistance is a difficult but not an endless undertaking. Some countries already have become self-reliant and are beginning to help others; U.S. policies should aim at hastening this process.

U.S. international development programs should be independent of U.S. military and economic programs that provide assistance for security purposes. Both types of programs are essential, but each serves a different purpose. Confusing them in concept and connecting them in administration detract from the effectiveness of both.

The United States should help make development a truly international effort. A new environment exists: other industrial countries are now doing more, international organizations can take on greater responsibilities, trade and private investments are more active elements in development, and, most important, the developing countries have gained experience and competence. Recognizing these conditions, the United States should redesign its policies so that

—the developing countries stand at the center of the international development effort, establishing their own priorities and receiving assistance in relation to the efforts they are making on their own behalf;

—the international lending institutions become the major channel for development assistance; and

—U.S. bilateral assistance is provided largely within a framework set by the international organizations.

U.S. international development policies should seek to widen the use of private initiative, private skills, and private resources in the developing countries. The experience of industrial countries and of the currently developing nations demonstrates that rapid growth is usually associated with a dynamic private sector.

Development is more than economic growth. Popular participation and the dispersion of the benefits of development among all groups in society are essential to the building of dynamic and healthy nations. U.S. development policies should contribute to this end.

While the Task Force shares the aspirations of many who have endorsed high targets for development assistance, we have deliberately decided against recommending any specific annual level of U.S. assistance or any formula for determining how much it should be. We do not believe that it is possible to forecast with any assurance what volume of external resources will be needed five to ten years hence. No single formula can encompass all that must be done—in trade, in investment, and in the quality as well as the amount of assistance. Our recommendation is to establish a framework of principles, procedures, and institutions that will assure the effective use of assistance funds and the achievement of U.S. national interests.

The downward trend in U.S. development assistance appropriations should be reversed. Additional resources, primarily in support of international lending institutions, are needed now for a new approach to international development. We believe this, having fully in mind the current financial stringency and urgent domestic priorities in the United States, as well as this country's balance-of-payments position. Over the long term, U.S. assistance for development abroad will be small in relation to expenditures for development at home. Moreover, the two programs can prove to be mutually reinforcing.

To carry out these policies, the Task Force recommends a new focus for U.S. programs, a new emphasis on multilateral organizations, and a new institutional framework.

Underlying the recommendations made by the task force was its belief that "International Development Assistance serves long-term U.S. national interests." It saw this interest as being derived from the fact that, "The developing countries contain two-thirds of the world's population and their future success or failure will influence profoundly the kind of world [U.S. citizens] live in." As they put it: "The nations of the world are growing more interdependent—in trade, in finance, in technology, and in the critical area of political change. U.S. decision-making in such important areas as military expenditures will be influenced by the amounts of turbulence in the developing countries of the world, and U.S. prosperity will be influenced by their economic progress."

In a fundamental sense the Peterson Task Force's report can be read as its advice to the President on how to sell to Congress and, to the limited extent that it matters, the public, requests for aid funds, whatever their real purpose. This public relations function was clearly illustrated when, after discussions with his political advisers and executive staff, President Nixon, on September 15, 1970, sent a message to Congress outlining his plans for a reform of the U.S. aid program. When asked, "Do you think the President's message will be successful in gaining support for foreign aid?" the deputy administrator (Mr. Marius Williams) of the U.S. aid agency—the Agency for International Development (AID)—replied, "Yes I think so . . . The AID program has lost effectiveness . . . in terms of public and Congressional support . . . AID no longer has effective support in the Congress and in the minds of the American people . . . Its role and function have become blurred . . . The President's message seeks to focus the attention of the American people on the importance of a substantial effort of assistance to help the low-income countries. The message provides a sound basis for building a new program and mechanisms where purposes and programs are clearly understood by Congress and the American people." [5]

Like the Peterson Report, on which it was largely based, the President's full message derived much of its logic from fear of the unspecified consequences of a failure to secure world peace. "Because [the low-income countries] contain two-thirds of the world's population, the direction which the development of their societies takes will profoundly affect the world in which we live.

[5] As reported in *Front Lines* (Washington, D.C.: AID Publication, September 24, 1970), page 3.

We must respond to the needs of those countries if our own country and its values are to remain secure . . . But foreign aid must be seen for what it is—not a burden, but an opportunity to help others to fulfill their aspirations for justice, dignity, and a better life. No more abroad than at home can peace be achieved and maintained without vigorous efforts to meet the needs of the less fortunate." [6] These sentiments were drawn on again when, after an unprecedented delay of seven months (during which the President and his advisers consulted with "Congress, the business community and many other sectors of the American public and our friends"), the President submitted to Congress on April 21, 1971, his draft of the legislation on the U.S. aid program which he was requesting Congress to approve.

In his transmittal message the President extended these sentiments, however, by itemizing in more detail the potential threats to U.S. interests and by directly countering some of the more prevalent criticisms of the aid program. In the preamble to his message accompanying the proposed legislation he argued: "The prospects for a peaceful world will be greatly enhanced if the two-thirds of humanity who live in [poor] countries see hope for adequate food, shelter, education and employment in peaceful progress *rather than in revolution.*" [7] The implication is that aid can help insure "peaceful progress," whatever that means. After outlining the institutional reforms and aid funds he was requesting, the President went on to "recognize that whenever an American firm is nationalized without prompt, fair, and effective compensation, whenever an anti-American demonstration takes place, or whenever a leader of a developing country criticizes the United States, many question the effectiveness of aid." The President asked such critics to take into account the "many countries who do thank us for providing them the means to preserve their own security; . . . the countless number of villages where farmers do appreciate our helping to provide the

[6] Ibid., page 4.

[7] This and the following quotations are from "Message from the President of the United States Transmitting Draft Legislation on Foreign Aid," House of Representatives Document No. 92–94 (April 21, 1971), page 2.

know-how and the tools necessary to grow larger crops . . . The school children who cherish the education our assistance makes possible, and the people everywhere who recognize our help in eliminating disease." While the President felt it necessary to point to the fact that "such appreciation is gratifying," he also argued, in seeking support for his proposed legislation, that, "foreign assistance has a *more basic purpose.*" This "more basic purpose" is to insure that "peace and prosperity for ourselves" which cannot be sustained, "if our friends cannot defend themselves against aggression, and if two-thirds of the world's people see the richer third as indifferent to their needs and insensitive to their aspirations for a better life." The President continued, "We cannot ask the lower income countries of the world to co-operate with us to solve the problems which affect *our vital interests* unless we cooperate with them to solve the problems critical to their vital interests." The President, then, was trying to gain congressional support for his requests for aid funds and reforms in the aid program, by arguing that aid was not only morally good in itself but, more importantly, also a price to be paid in order to insure that the recipient countries respect and enhance various "interests" (never clearly specified) of the United States.

I have devoted a lot of space to the early stages of the formation of U.S. aid legislation, because it is at this stage that the President attempts to assess public and congressional opinion and base his justification for his requests for aid on that assessment, regardless of what the President feels to be the real justification. When the proposed legislation reaches Congress it is "read" on the floors of both the Senate and the House of Representatives and then referred to their respective subcommittees for debate. These subcommittees—the Foreign Relations Committee of the Senate and the Foreign Affairs Committee (for bilateral and voluntary international aid) of the House—are charged with advising their respective chambers as to what action should be taken on the President's proposals. The President must take two key political factors into account when making his requests: first the state of relations between himself and Congress; and second, the state of opinion in Congress. If the President misjudges the state of that opinion, then the committees are likely to recommend amendments to, or rejection of, the President's proposals. And, as the Senate and House are not bound by the recommendations of their subcommittees, they also may decide to amend or reject the President's proposals. Regardless of opinion on aid in Congress, if the President fails to maintain good relations with Congress, there is an additional possibility that his proposals may be rejected, amended, or delayed because members of Congress do not themselves feel the questions under discussion to be of pressing importance to their own interests. It is clear that in 1971 the President miscalculated the situation with respect to both factors and, while the details of the resulting debate are not important to our purpose here, the mechanics of it can be used to throw light on the domestic politics of aid.

When the bills containing the President's aid proposals reached the congressional committees in April, they met with a hostile reception. This was partly because Congress, already hostile toward the Executive for other reasons, felt annoyed because, owing to the seven-month delay between the President's September message and the arrival of the aid bill, they were requested to pass major legislation concerning the reform of the U.S. aid program without adequate time in which to examine it. It was partly due also to the simple fact that a majority of the members of Congress did not accept the arguments which the President used to justify the proposals. When such a situation arises the President will, if he considers the proposed legislation an important component of his total policy, bring considerable political pressure to bear on members of Congress in order to gain their support. In this case he did not. As Representatives Gross, Derwinski, and Thompson put it in their minority report in the House Foreign Affairs Committee:

"The Executive didn't have the heart to push it." Their implication was that the President did not consider his aid proposals
to be of sufficient political importance to merit his putting pressure on Congress to approve them. At any one time a President
will concentrate his political guns on objectives of importance
to him; the aid bills were not. Thus, the argument made
earlier that aid lacks strong leadership in the United States was
supported in this instance.

When the aid bills reached the congressional committees, they
quickly decided they would not proceed with them as they stood
—containing the President's proposals for reform—and agreed to
debate only a continuing bill, maintaining the existing machinery
and indicating the funds they would be prepared to make available to it for the following fiscal year. At this stage public
opinion at large counts, in general, for little or nothing. Congressmen receive little mail concerning aid, and, for the most
part, their constituents do not attempt directly to influence their
representatives while they are debating aid bills. But lobbies
and other interest groups, both pro- and antiaid, can and do
enter the scene at this stage, by taking advantage of the hearings system which allows them to make their case publicly
to the committees and to have their views printed in the
Congressional Record. All the lobbyists' tactics are then drawn
on in the attempt to influence congressional opinion. In addition, the committee stage allows Congressmen to participate
directly in the construction of proposals for legislation in response to the President's requests and to state publicly their
own opinions. For some, the discussions on the aid bill are
important, as this is one of the few areas in which their opinion
on U.S. foreign relations and policy can be expressed. Little
purpose would be served here by going into the question of
the effects of specific lobbies on congressional opinion. We
might, however, note that the record shows that few Congressmen display deep concern for the underlying problem of the
acute poverty of the majority of citizens in poor countries.

It is the collective opinion of the committees which determines what form the bill takes when reported back to their respective chambers for discussion and action. The individual opinions of committee members, reflecting their own views or those of interest groups whose support they want, can only affect the form of the draft bill if they are shared by a majority of their committee. At any given time committees do tend to have collective views, which are reflected in their reaction to proposals put to them by the President, the Administration, interest groups, and their own individual members. We have already noted the consequences of the feeling of near-hostility toward the President which characterized Congress as a whole in 1971. We can go beyond that and examine, briefly, the consequences both of the conservatism which characterized the House Committee on Foreign Affairs and of the "anti-involvement" liberalism of the Senate Committee on Foreign Relations in 1971. The conservatism of the House committee can be seen in its tendency to regard aid as primarily serving the domestic interests of the United States and in its advocacy (contrary to the President's wishes) of the maintenance at its present level, or even increase, of the bilateral aid program. The Senior Staff Consultant to the committee, Roy J. Bullock, probably caught the mood of the majority of its members when he wrote, "Instead of directing U.S. foreign policy and U.S. assistance toward producing a world of independent countries each free to go its own way, it would be to our advantage to give priority to the development of relationships of mutual confidence and a feeling that foreign nations benefit from being dependent in a greater or less degree on us, and that we benefit from our association with them." [8]

The Senate committee's majority opinion was that such dependence necessarily implies undesirable involvement in the

[8] From "Staff Memorandum on What to Do about Foreign Aid," House of Representatives Committee on Foreign Affairs (March 24, 1969), page 9.

internal affairs of recipient countries; and Vietnam was never far from the minds of the more liberal members of the Senate. In contrast to the House committee's emphasis on the short-term bilateral benefits of aid, the Senate committee majority view was that the main value of aid lies in the longer run, in the more peaceful, and, thus, secure world they believe it is capable of achieving. Added to this were the prevailing views in the Senate that international agencies are not as efficient as they might be and that the transfer currently involved in aid is in reality from the poorer taxpayer in the U.S. to the richer sections of the recipient countries' population. The Senate committee generally welcomed the President's proposals for an increased multilateral element in U.S. aid but deprecated his request for an expanded bilateral program. They would have preferred a smaller absolute program with a larger proportion allocated to international agencies, with mechanisms for securing its efficient use. Thus, the Senate committee's reaction to the President's proposals was more or less the exact opposite to that of the House committee.

The actual details of the 1971 controversies over aid legislation are less important here than the illustration of how the constitutional system in the U.S. creates confrontation situations. In such situations differences of opinion can severely hamper progress on legislation, while the President and the two Houses of Congress all hold out for legislation which reflects their own view. In 1971 the aid legislation was very much affected by the tripartite division of authority. It was affected also by the division in the House of Representatives of responsibility for bilateral and multilateral aid between its Committees on Foreign Affairs and Currency and Banking, respectively. Another important institutional factor which was present in 1971 was congressional distrust of the Administration. Two issues in particular aroused antagonistic feelings toward aid in Congress. In the first place Congress felt that the Administration placed too much emphasis on military assistance; in fact, requests for military aid funds by the Administration were in excess of those requested for development and humanitarian purposes. And, second, Congress felt that the U.S. AID branch of the Administration was too technocratic and professional in its approach to development assistance and was proposing policies and programs (especially aid for Greece) which were (or were potentially) inconsistent with overall U.S. foreign policy.

In summary, the President sent draft legislation to Congress proposing a shift toward multilateralization, new bilateral institutions, and a modest increase in total funds. The House Committee on Foreign Affairs refused to discuss the proposed institutional reform and sent a draft bill to the House which proposed a strengthening of the bilateral program involving allocations of more funds than requested by the President. This bill was accepted and passed by the House in August. The House Currency and Banking Committee was not so cooperative with, in separate bills, proposed allocations to the aid arm of the World Bank—the International Development Association (IDA)—and the regional development banks for Latin America and Asia. This partly reflected House disillusionment with the efficiency of international agencies, but mostly their feeling was that "bilateral is better" and that more of IDA's funds should come from European countries and be seen to benefit the United States. At the same time the Senate (having passed the allocation for international institutions) passed a bill which cut back severely President Nixon's request for bilateral funds and ignored his proposed institutional reforms.

With such divergent starting points it was several months before the Senate and House could agree on a compromise aid bill. The U.S. aid program was only able to continue in existence over that period by the passing of "continuing resolutions," which provided for funding of the program on a day-to-day basis. The Act that was eventually passed completely ignored the President's proposals for institutional reforms and cut back heavily on the amount of funds made available vis-à-vis both the amount the President requested and the amounts provided in the preceding years.

Conclusion

Although this chapter has concentrated on the situation in the United States, the domestic politics of aid in that country are a fairly accurate indication of the situation prevailing in all donor countries, although the systems by which attitudes are transformed into action by legislative processes obviously differ from country to country. The first conclusion is that, for several reasons, the public at large is ignorant about the actual nature of their countries' aid programs, believing them to represent a larger sacrifice (burden) than they do, in fact, constitute. They are encouraged in this belief by the international rhetoric of aid. Taking this in conjunction with general antagonism toward taxes and the tendency of news media to concentrate on the failures rather than the successes of aid, it is not surprising that the majority of taxpayers in donor countries are "against" aid. This general antipathy toward aid is strengthened when poor countries begin to be able to compete economically with some industries in the donor countries.

The second conclusion of the chapter is that while aid programs can operate more or less independently of the state of public opinion (because of their relative unimportance in the spectrum of domestic political issues), they *are not* independent of domestic political battles which are totally unrelated to the economic situation of the mass of inhabitants of the Third World. In the absence of strong political leadership, aid programs are vulnerable to administrators and politicians who wish to use them to serve their own political ends—to provide favors to specific groups of people, to support an image as a taxpayers' guardian, or to attempt to influence world events in some small way.

The process by which an aid program can be transformed from a recognition of international responsibility toward the Third World into a reflection only of domestic political forces was illustrated by a description of the passage of the 1972 U.S. aid bill through that country's legislative processes. In the United States it is the responsibility of the President to insure that aid legislation is consistent with overall government policy. That policy, as the President has stressed on several occasions, incorporates a recognition of the need for an increased aid effort on the part of the United States; this need is derived from the belief that the amelioration of poverty in the Third World is in the United States's own self-interest. Inconsistently, however, President Nixon did not, in 1971, take the necessary initiatives to insure that the U.S. aid program reflected his statements of the U.S. interest in helping poor countries to develop. In fact, in his August 15 economic crisis policy package he displayed a lack of concern for the problems of less-developed countries by reducing 1971–1972 aid disbursements by 10 percent, by raising tariffs on imports by 10 percent, and by effectively devaluing the reserves of poor countries by lowering the exchange value of the dollar in those reserves without compensation.

The overall conclusion of this and the previous chapter is, then, that aid programs of donor countries represent the juxtaposition of an identification of donor self-interest in the provision of aid and domestic political forces which are divorced from any concept of a need of poor countries for aid. The next chapter discusses the possibility of quantitatively measuring the extent of this need.

V

HOW MUCH AID IS NEEDED?

Faced with claims from poor countries that they are in need of aid, naturally the rich countries ask, "How much?" Any figure which is put up in response to this counterquestion has to have provided with it the reasoning which has been used to arrive at it. If the figure is acceptable to them, the supporters of the poor countries' claims will take a political stand on it and tend to ignore the defects in the reasoning on which it is based. This, too, is only natural. But it is also dangerous. It is dangerous first because the defects in the reasoning are easily exposed to destructive criticism. Second, it implies that the growth process is sufficiently well understood for us to be able to calculate how much aid is required to achieve given rates of economic growth, and it implicitly equates such growth with socially desirable development, which may not be valid. The existence of these dangers will become apparent as this chapter proceeds.

In the next section the possibility of scientifically calculating the aid needs of poor countries is discussed and dismissed as unrealistic and unnecessary. It is unnecessary because the aid needs of poor countries are unlimited. In the section following this discussion the point is made that although the aid needs of poor countries are conceptually unlimited, there are, in fact, limits to their capacity to absorb (i.e. usefully employ) aid. Neither the need for nor the capacity to absorb aid represents the demand of poor countries for aid. Once the economic and political price demanded by rich countries for aid is allowed for, a poor country's effective demand for aid may be considerably less than its need or its absorptive capacity. This chapter concludes by arguing that even at its going price the total effective demand for aid by poor countries is considerably in excess of the amounts made available by the rich countries. Thus the flows of aid from rich to poor are supply-determined and bear little or no relation to any concept of need.

Can Aid Needs Be Calculated?

In recent years, several attempts have been made to calculate an overall figure for the aid needs of less-developed countries. In this section the logic of such calculations is first examined and then criticized, using one specific example of such a calculation.[1] There is a common tendency in the literature on poor countries to equate economic growth with development and, thus, to take the objective of maximizing the rate of development to mean maximizing the rate of economic growth. Such simplifying assumptions can be used to extend the subtitle question to: How can we calculate how much aid is needed to maximize the rate of economic growth in a country? Even though this question is more manageable, in that it is in terms of factors which are quantifiable, it is still not easy to provide a simple answer. It was argued in a preceding chapter that no one

[1] The example discussed in this section is that prepared by the Secretariat of UNCTAD for its second session in New Delhi in 1968, *Trade Prospects and Capital Needs of Developing Countries* (New York: United Nations, 1968). UN Sales No. E.68.II.D.13. Other examples are the estimates made in Bela Balassa, *Trade Prospects for Developing Countries* (Homewood, Ill.: Richard Irwin, 1964); "General Agreement on Tariffs and Trade," *International Trade 1961* (Geneva, 1962); United Nations, *World Economic Survey 1962* (New York, 1963); International Bank for Reconstruction and Development, *Annual Report 1964–1965* (Washington, D.C.: IBRD, 1965); and I. M. D. Little and J. M. Clifford, *International Aid* (London: Allen and Unwin, 1965).

really understands exactly how economies function and thus, a fortiori, no one knows for certain what policies to follow in order to maximize growth. It follows that recipients cannot know precisely how much aid to request or precisely what forms of aid to seek in order to achieve an objective such as maximizing the rate of economic growth.

It is not, however, being argued here that since governments do not know what are the "best" policies to follow or what will be the precise effects of the policies they do follow, they should not seek any aid at all. All governments have to plan their policies, even if only on a year-to-year basis as in most developed countries. Broadly speaking there are two ways to approach such planning. The first approach begins with the government estimating the resources the country is likely to have available in a given period and then devising a program of policies which will allocate the resources in such a way as is thought would maximize growth. The second approach starts by setting a target rate of growth, which it is hoped the economy can achieve, and then estimating the inputs and outputs which would be required of the various sections of the economy in order to achieve that rate.

Both approaches depend on simulating in some way the actual economic relationships at play in the economy. The second approach will define an amount of aid required to sustain the desired rate of growth, given the nature of the simulation. In the first approach the simulation will determine the maximum rate of growth which can be attained on the basis of the estimate of available resources and at the same time show how aid-financed resource flows could augment that rate of growth. Clearly, in both cases the nature of the simulation of the economy is crucial.

Simulation, or model building, as it is usually called, is the job of the economist. An economic system consists of a set of behavioral relationships which determine how resources are allocated among the various possible users and how final products are distributed among consumers. The behavioral relationships can be determined by the government, or in an open market in which the participants are activated by self-interest, or by some mixture of the two. If it is difficult for a government to estimate what resources will be available in its economy over a given period, it is virtually impossible for it to identify and assess the relative strengths of all the behavioral forces at play. No one can accurately represent the totality of an economy on paper or in a computer program. The real world is just too complex for that. All the economist can do is attempt to devise a model of the economy which correctly identifies the relationships which have a major influence on the level and direction of economic activities. If he is correct in his specification of the model, the economist can then indicate to the government how the resources expected to be available should be allocated, to try to achieve whatever set of objectives the government has devised for the country. Or the economist could take as data the set of objectives desired by the government and use his model to estimate the resources required to achieve them.

Economic systems are not, however, static. Attitudes, tastes, ambitions, and the political aims of dominant groups change continuously and, in doing so, affect the relative strength of the various forces at play in the economy. Similarly, over time, resource availabilities change and the technical coefficients which determine their productivity in different uses also change. The economist has to attempt to predict these changes if his models, and the prescriptions derived from them, are to be realistic. Realism also demands that these models take into account the possibility of stochastic impacts on the system occurring due to wars, diseases, freak weather, other natural catastrophes, and political upheavals. It will be clear that, on the basis of the present state of economic science, impossible demands are being made of the economist. First, the calculation of a figure for aid needed by a country can only be as accurate as the model used is realistic. Second, "need" is obviously defined in such a context with reference to the set of objectives specified by the government of the country. Such calculations are extremely sensitive to quite minor variations in the assumptions of the model and in the targets set by the government.

Many governments and international organizations, however, use such models. One was used by the Secretariat of the United Nations Conference on Trade and Development (UNCTAD) in order to present the second session of the Conference (held in New Delhi, March–April 1968) with an estimate of the aid needs of less-developed countries. The model used by UNCTAD was of the simplest possible kind. Setting two targets (a high and a low) for the rate of economic growth (Gross Domestic Product), and on the basis of set assumptions concerning the capital and import intensities of output, estimates were derived for the rates of growth of imports required to sustain the growth targets. Projections were then made for the rate of growth of exports. Projected export earnings were deducted from import requirements to arrive at figures for export-import gaps for each less-developed country. The export-import gap represents the amount of additional foreign exchange required to sustain the target rates of growth on the given assumptions. This gap does not alone measure the aid requirements of the individual countries. To this gap must be added the "invisible" gap, that is, the shortfall between receipts and expenditures for and on services and autonomous movements of capital. It proved impossible to estimate this invisible gap for the individual less-developed countries, so to the sum of export-import gaps the Secretariat added an estimate of the invisible gap for the Third World as a whole. The sum of the two gaps was called the trade gap. This gap is, on the given assumptions, the difference between the projected import requirements of the Third World in 1975 and its capacity to finance such imports out of the resources of its own that it was projected it will have that year.

The trade gap of this model does not measure aid needs, although the UNCTAD document claimed, on the basis of the maximum projected gap of $26 billion (using all upper-limit assumptions), that: "The total *required* inflow of public and private capital would *thus* amount to $18 billion." [2] The emphasis on the words "required" and "thus" is mine; in the document these categorical words are based on two *conditional* statements. First, "If one half of the trade gap *were to be* bridged by public capital inflow (on average terms approximately the same as those prevailing in 1965), this model *would* involve an increase in such inflow to some $13 billion net by 1975." And second, "It *may also be* anticipated that private capital inflow *would* [*sic*] rise to $5 billion by 1975." The emphasis is again mine, but the illegitimate translation of the conditional into the categorical is theirs. The document indicates, without any mention of the problems involved, that the "remainder of the gap would probably have to be bridged by a higher rate of import substitution than in the past."

Projections of trade gaps are irrelevant to the problem of estimating aid needs of less-developed countries. In this model they are simply *defined* as the difference between the effects of policy changes (designed to increase import substitution) and commercially determined capital flows. There is no economic justification of such a definition; in the UNCTAD document it is simply pulled out of the air as a result of the illegitimate deduction of a categorical statement from conditional premises. The authors of the technical section of the document are clearly aware of the limitations of their work when they say:

It should be emphasized that projections, like forecasts, are subject to error, which would affect the estimates of the dependent quantities even if the assumed developments took place. These errors arise from the necessity of using statistical methods and from the occurrence of unexpected structural changes in the basic relationships. In short, the estimates given in this study of the relationships between the variables are essentially estimates of the most probable values; consequently, the estimates of the dependent quantities (e.g. foreign exchange gaps) are estimates of the most

[2] Secretariat of UNCTAD, *Trade Prospects and Capital Needs of Developing Countries*, page 6.

probable outcomes which would be expected if the specified 'exogenous' assumptions proved valid. Obviously if they do not prove valid (e.g. if the growth rate of developing countries were different from the projected rate), the dependent outcomes can no longer be expected. However, even if all the assumptions, in the event, prove correct, the dependent estimates could still go wrong because the estimates of the structural relationships by which the latter have been derived from the former are themselves subject to error.[3]

The trouble is that those people who are not aware of the technical difficulties involved in such work tend to ignore such warnings. Indeed, in the preface to the UNCTAD study, Raul Prebisch, the then Secretary General of UNCTAD, says, "The study . . . *shows* that if the developed countries were prepared to supply 1 percent of their gross national products, this would go far towards meeting the requirements for a 6 percent coverage rate of growth in developing countries. *Thus* the study provides a *solid base* for the elaboration of new national and international targets for the United Nations Development Decade of the 1970s." [4] The study provides, as its authors correctly point out, no justification for such claims. In fact, the study throws no light at all on the question of how much aid less-developed countries need.

The Need for Aid Is Extremely High

Models such as that used by UNCTAD do usefully draw attention to the impossibility of less-developed countries achieving even modest rates of growth on the basis of the resources available to them, before any aid is allowed for. Taking the less-developed world as a whole, assuming the growth prospects and economic policies toward the less-developed countries of the developed countries are fixed, and making the most optimistic assumptions concerning the technical coefficients at

[3] Ibid., page 9.
[4] Ibid., page iii.

every stage, it is unlikely that they could do much more than prevent a decline in their per capita income on the basis of their own resources for the foreseeable future. To achieve any more than this, aid must be extended to them by the developed countries.

The scale of poverty which exists in the Third World is such that it is impossible to look forward to its eradication within the next hundred years. For example, it would take India one hundred years growth at about 4 percent per capita per annum to achieve per capita income around $4,000. This is roughly that found in the United States today, where poverty has not yet been eradicated. It would also involve a gross growth rate of around 7 percent, which is generally considered well beyond the capacity of India to sustain on the basis of its own resources. Indeed, few countries have ever been able to obtain such a growth rate, even for a short period. Even if the developed countries supplied the largest figure for the trade gap, estimated by UNCTAD for 1975 as $26 billion, as outright gifts, conditions of abject poverty would still prevail throughout the Third World. People who are ill-fed, ill-housed, and poorly educated can always and will always be able to "usefully employ" aid in order to survive and improve their lot. Aid can also be usefully employed in order to support the consumption needs of their children in the future. In the context of the models, however, "usefully employ" refers to the amount of additional investable resources which can be employed in the economy to generate consumption streams in the future, without any consideration being given to the relevant weights to be placed on present versus future real basic human needs. To label such amounts, determined by ivory-tower technicians on tentative and arbitrary assumptions, as representing the "needs" of the people of the less-developed countries is a travesty.

Aid could consist solely of additions to the current consumption of the poor people in the Third World. That is, programs could be devised which transferred supplies of consumption goods from the rich countries to the poor sections of the Third

World and investment there financed entirely out of their own resources. There can be little doubt that a vast amount, far in excess of current levels, could be so transferred before the loss in welfare to the taxpayer of the rich countries ceased to be outweighed by the gain in welfare to the inhabitants of the Third World. Transfers sufficient to equate welfare from current consumption at the margin would probably be totally unacceptable to those taxed to provide them. The more resources that are devoted to current consumption, the less there are to devote to investment in uses which would generate future streams of consumption goods and services.

Investment can be regarded as a tax on consumers today in order to ensure the welfare of consumers tomorrow. And the analogue of the dilemma over international transfers is the dilemma within less-developed countries concerning transfers from consumers today to consumers tomorrow. If the governments of less-developed countries are unable, on the basis of existing resources at their command, to guarantee satisfactory living conditions and consumption standards to their present citizens, then a fortiori they are unable to divert sufficient resources away from current consumption in order to secure the conditions and standards they would like to see their descendants enjoy. Aid eases this dilemma by adding to the resources available for consumption or investment or both. But if the amount of such resources required to equalize welfare from current consumption would be immense, then the amount of aid required to generate sufficient investment in less-developed countries to equalize welfare from consumption streams in the future would be astronomical. This is so for two reasons. In the first place, the standard of living in rich countries is rising much more rapidly than it is in poor countries so that the transfer required to equalize welfare in both groups of countries is increasing over time. And second, population is growing more rapidly in poor countries so that the growth in their income has to be divided more extensively: thus, even more investment now is required to provide the desired higher standard of living for the future expansion of population. If the amount of income transfers necessary to equalize welfare from current consumption is politically unacceptable, then the larger amount required to guarantee future equalization of welfare is beyond consideration.

The Limits to Poor Countries' Capacity to Absorb Aid

The concept of absorptive capacity has not been much used by professionals in recent years, largely because of the difficulty of giving it a quantifiable meaning on an aggregative basis. The concept derives from a basic principle of economic theory, known as the law of diminishing returns. This law says that if the supply of one factor used in production is increased, while the supplies of all other factors remain constant, the returns (in terms of increased output) to the increasing factor may at first increase but will eventually begin to decline and at some point turn negative. If aid is regarded as a single factor then there should, conceptually, be some optimum flow of aid defined in terms of its return from the use to which the recipients put it, balanced against the opportunity cost (foregone returns) resulting from the donors not using the aid-financed resources in some other way. It is impossible, however, to estimate with any acceptable degree of accuracy the expected return on flows of aid to a given country. Difficulties arise because aid is not a single factor—it can be anything produced in donor countries —and the optimum total of aid would have to be calculated by adding up the amounts of all types of resources needed to equate returns in all possible uses. Obviously, the total requirements figure varies with the rate of return aimed at in the various activities. Thus, a policy of increasing investment in all possible uses up to a point where the rate of return was only 1 percent of the marginal investment would call for far more aid than would a policy based on a target rate of return of 10 percent. Furthermore, there is no unambiguous method for measuring returns; some "products" cannot be measured meaningfully in purely economic terms, for example, the returns to expenditure on cultural activities or defense. Another complication is added by considering the aid needs of different countries: a rate of return of 10 percent may have a much higher welfare content in a very poor country than it would have in a relatively rich country, thus making it difficult to determine the optimum distribution of aid among recipients.

Even though it does not give us any definite answers to the question of how much aid poor countries need, the concept of absorptive capacity does have considerable intuitive appeal. Clearly, at any given time there is an ultimate limit to the amount of physical resources that each poor country can cope with. Let us, once again, take an extreme example to make the point. Assume that all aid to a certain country takes the form of tractors and that the tractors can only be transported to that country by sea. It requires little imagination to appreciate that there is a physical limit to the number of tractors that can be shipped through given port facilities in, say, a year. Anyone who has witnessed such scenes as ships carrying aid-financed goods lining up to enter Colombo (Ceylon) harbor or such goods lying idle in the warehouses of Callao port (Peru) will not question the assertion. But docks and attendant facilities are not the only factor impinging on a country's capacity to absorb aid. Each tractor imported requires that there be a trained tractor driver to operate it. Thus, the supply of such operators is another limit to the country's ability to absorb tractors. Similarly, the country's internal transport facilities, methods of distribution among potential users, and stock of farmers with methods and abilities such that they could usefully employ tractors, also limit the capacity of the country to absorb aid. The absorption approach is, then, more realistic than models such as that used by UNCTAD in that it explicitly recognizes that other factors besides a simple shortage of investment goods can constrain the level of growth which can be achieved; that is, it admits the very real possibility that there is some physical limit to the amount of investment goods that can be absorbed in any period. This limit is defined by the amount of complementary resources which are available, although this will vary among the different possible uses for the investment goods. However, even if all investment projects were undertaken in all recipient countries up to the point where no more complementary resources were available—regardless of the marginal rate of return—it still would not necessarily be correct to say that all their needs for aid were satisfied. It would still be possible to use aid to subsidize the consumption levels of existing poor people.

Even if all the world's immediately investable resources were distributed equally among the world's population via a massive aid program, consumption aid would be required to bring the poor countries nearer to the average standard of living considered adequate in the donor countries today. To say that the distribution channels and complementary factors of production currently available would limit the ability of donors and recipients to manage such an aid program is not to deny that the gap between rich and poor countries exists. It only indicates that there is a limit to the world's ability to narrow or close that gap. That limit is, however, far from being reached today; and by using this notion of a limit as a definition of absorptive capacity, we can say that it is more than likely that less-developed countries could absorb far more aid than the donor countries are ever likely to supply.

The Limits to Poor Countries' Demand for Aid

So far in this chapter I have used the word "aid" as if it referred to an unrequited flow of resources from rich to poor countries—that is, as a free good to recipient countries. If that were the case in practice then we would expect poor countries to demand aid up to the point where it was physically impossible for them to handle any more. But aid is not a free good: the acceptance of aid imposes costs on the recipient. In the first place donors (both national governments and international agencies) require recipients to demonstrate that aid will be used in ways regarded by donors as "worthwhile." Various criteria have been devised by donors for determining whether a proposal, made by recipients in order to justify the receipt of aid, can be classed as worthwhile. Recipients thus have to allocate resources (educated manpower and ancillary resources) and time to preparing and presenting such proposals. A more important cost to the recipient may result from the biasing of development plans by recipients away from their preferred objectives in order to justify larger allocations of aid.

Second, most aid takes the form of loans and not outright grants. The cost of accepting aid in the form of a loan is the commitment to repay it with interest in the future. We have seen in Chapter 2 the heavy and increasing price which poor countries are now paying for past aid loans. Estimates of future ability to repay loans will obviously provide a limit to a country's willingness to accept loans now. Furthermore, as loan repayments and interest charges have to be made in foreign exchange, recipients may be swayed in their development planning to allocate more resources to activities which will save on or generate future foreign exchange flows in order to be able to accept more aid now. Such distortions in planning may run counter to social objectives; and when they do, they must be counted as a further cost of accepting aid.

A third important cost of some aid is that donors frequently make aid conditional on recipients providing services to the donors. There are many examples of such conditions being attached to aid, either explicitly or implicitly. Implicit in the provision of all U.S. aid, for example, is the condition that the recipient government be considered acceptable in its politics by the U.S. government. Other examples are international support for the foreign policies of donors; the provision of military bases; the provision of troops; the acceptance of private investment by donor-based businesses; and even the surrender of some sovereignty in terms of the determination of the form of economic and social policies followed by the recipients. Finally, most donors require aid to be spent on goods and services produced and provided by their nationals, and in such cases the cost to recipients of such goods and services is frequently above their market prices.

Aid, therefore, is not a free good to recipients. The conditions on which aid is extended exact a price from recipients, and while demand for aid might be unlimited if no price at all were attached to it, there will obviously be a reduction in demand as the conditions on which aid is proffered become more onerous in the estimation of its recipients. Effective demand for aid, then, is a function of its "cost" to the recipient.

The Market for Aid

Before an aid flow can take place, two parties—a donor and a recipient—have to agree to the transaction. If a donor government is to agree to supply aid, it has to be satisfied that the (economic and political) costs involved in raising the funds are balanced by the returns it gets from allocating them to poor countries. In preceding chapters I have discussed the nature of the returns donors seek from their aid programs. Recipients, in turn, have to be satisfied that the benefits they expect to accrue from accepting aid are greater than the costs imposed on them by the conditions attached to its acceptance. While recipient countries naturally press for reductions in the cost of aid, we know from their statements in the various international forums that they would be willing to accept flows of aid at their current "price" considerably in excess of this current level.

In a situation in which the demand for aid exceeds its supply, the aid problem has two operational facets: the determinants of its distribution among potential recipients, and the determinants of its overall supply.

Ability to pay the highest monetary price (in terms of interest and speed of repayment) is not the only factor which donors take into account when deciding how to allocate their aid. In the last section and in preceding chapters I have identified other factors which donors take into account. For example, ability to contribute to the donor's sense of security, willingness to give diplomatic support to donors, and provision of facilities to donor-based private interests have been identified as services which donors have shown themselves willing to accept in return for aid. Poor countries which can and are willing to provide such services are more likely to receive aid than those which cannot or will not. The evidence supports this hypothesis. Thus, aid from a country which has declared itself as being opposed to the spread of communist influence (the United States for example) is more likely to be provided to countries which show themselves willing to oppose the spread of such influence (e.g. South Vietnam, Turkey, Taiwan, and South Korea) than to countries which do not (e.g. Tanzania, Albania, and Cuba).

The various stages on which international politics are played continuously display to the officials who formulate donor aid policies what "payments" they can receive in return for aid. Faced with this knowledge donor governments have to decide on the share of their countries' income which they wish to allocate to their aid programs. The major donors—France, Germany, the United Kingdom, and the United States—obviously consider that the returns they get from aid are dwindling in absolute and/or relative value, as over the last decade or so the proportion of their income which they allocate to aid has continuously fallen.

Decisions of individual donors about the size of the aid program are taken in the context of a changing international and domestic environment. Social and domestic problems and the political pressures they give rise to seem to have grown in urgency and force in several donor countries over the 1960s. This has led to a diminution of the relative importance of aid programs in the minds of the officials concerned in rich countries. An apparent lessening of the kind of world tension which would have lead to a world war, splits in the communist bloc, and (following Algeria, Korea, South Vietnam, and Malaysia) an awareness of the increased cost of overseas military involvement were among several international factors which led to a feeling that "buying" the support of poor countries with aid was an expensive way to pay for a rather shaky sense of security. We saw in previous chapters how such factors based on the security motives enter into the domestic politics of aid and affect a country's overall willingness to mount aid programs. Economic factors we have already noted which have lessened support for aid in donor countries have been increased competition with poor countries for domestic and foreign markets as their agriculture and industries grow in strength, and problems with the international monetary mechanism, both of which have led to a move toward isolationism among donors.

Conclusion

The amount of aid which would be required by the countries of the Third World in order to remove poverty among their inhabitants is incalculable by existing methods, but it is certainly beyond the capacity of the world economy to supply. Even the more limited amount the poor countries could physically and efficiently employ exceeds the amount the donor countries are willing to make available, given the returns they currently see as accruing to them from existing aid. At its going price there is excess demand for aid. The degree to which demand for aid exceeds its supply has been and is likely to go on increasing as the services which poor countries can perform for rich countries are valued less and less by the rich countries. For those of us whose support for aid derives solely from the humanitarian motive, it is essential that the amount of aid which donor governments do make available should be used as efficiently as possible. To this end, it is important first that those in control of the limited supplies of aid available should be professionally and technically competent and free from pressures from those who do not share our concern for the world's poor. Second, we must try to insure that the ways in which aid is provided maximize the contribution of that aid to the reduction of poverty. And, finally, we must try to insure that the aid funds available go to those countries where poverty is most extensive. These issues are taken up, in turn, in the next three chapters.

VI

CURRENT CONTROVERSIES
CONCERNING THE FORMS OF AID

There is a multitude of means by which concessionary international transfers of economic resources can be effected. This chapter is concerned with the analysis of the controversies surrounding some alternative methods of transfer. Two basic issues underlie most of these controversies. The first is that of leverage of the donors over the policies of recipients; the second is that of the inherent efficiency of the mechanisms in achieving the objectives of the donor, recipient, or both. A related, and equally important issue, concerns the degree to which aid flows should be directed by international organizations. This issue, which is not specifically concerned with the form aid takes, is discussed in the following chapter.

There are many ways in which one nation can assist the inhabitants of another to increase their economic welfare. Some ways which a country can use to provide aid to others are either not obvious or have not so far been tried; nevertheless, they, too, are focal points of controversy. In this chapter I have selected several aid mechanisms, obvious and obscure, tried and untried, for analysis. The issues selected are: (1) should resources be loaned or given away; (2) should aid be extended in the form of subsidies to private investors in the less-developed countries; (3) should aid be used to finance specific projects in less-developed countries or used to support their overall economic programs; (4) should aid be related to specific balance-of-payments problems of individual less-developed countries; (5) should product markets be so controlled as to effectively transfer resources to poor exporting countries; (6) should the international monetary mechanism be used as a method of directing aid to the poor countries; (7) how much emphasis, if any, should be placed on technical assistance as a form of aid; and (8) should an international tax be devised to accumulate funds for aid.

Advocates and critics of the various forms of aid take their stances for widely different reasons. People who are, in general, opposed to aid in any form may see some forms of aid as lesser evils, while others, who are generally in favor of aid, may have objections to specific forms it may take and the ways in which its use is controlled. Those who see the objective of aid as the encouragement of private enterprise in the world at large would be likely to prefer one of the subsidized private investment schemes. At the other extreme, those who feel that aid is or should be compensation for the exploitative practices of rich countries may prefer some form of transfer which minimizes the interference of rich countries in the affairs of poor countries. The decision as to what form aid transfers should take will depend on which of the many possible objectives of aid is held to be most important by those making the decision.

Grants versus Loans

If one's friend needs some cash, it may seem obvious that the best way in which one can help him is by giving him some of one's own, either as much as he needs or as much as one can afford. In this way one maximizes the value of the transfer of resources of a given monetary value. This is the simple and conclusive argument of those who believe that all international aid should take the form of gifts. Most aid actually takes the form of loans, reflecting the fact that those responsible for aid policy in the donor countries have not been persuaded by this argument. They object to it for a variety of reasons. One of the most frequently used antigrant arguments holds that gifts encourage financial irresponsibility on the part of the recipient. The rationale underlying this objection is that as whatever the recipient buys with the gift will have effectively cost it nothing, it will not be under any incentive to seek an adequate economic or social return from the gift. In other words, the requirement to repay aid imposes upon the recipient a degree of financial responsibility: they will be induced not to waste aid but to invest it "wisely," that is, in such a way as to generate at least enough income to repay the loan. The inevitable consequence of the predominant and increasing emphasis on aid in the form of loans is that less-developed countries need to divert increasing amounts of their net inflows of foreign exchange to pay interest and amortization charges on past loans. For many less-developed countries, indeed for the whole Third World, these reverse flows are approaching the point at which they will exceed new inflows of aid funds. As noted elsewhere in the book (Chapter 2), the debt-servicing problem is one of the most serious problems facing the world community. Meanwhile, the poor countries, with their desperate need for resources, are being forced to mortgage more and more of their future income in order to obtain essential foreign exchange now. Many of the purposes for which the less-developed countries require funds either have no monetary payoff (e.g. health) or payoff only in local currency which donors are not willing to accept in repayment of loans (e.g. education) or have extremely long payoff periods (e.g. roads). As a result they are increasingly forced to tax the importing sections of their economies in order to service past loans. As more and more of their free foreign exchange, earned from exporting, is given over to such service payments, they are forced to press for increasing amounts of aid to allow their economies to purchase necessary imports.

The objections of the antigrant lobby are invalid anyway. In the first place, this lobby falsely identifies fiscal responsibility with monetary returns. Most aid loans, however, are extended to the governments of less-developed countries, who, as implied in the last paragraph, may frequently base their investment decisions on expected *social* returns such as improvements in the health, literacy, and physical environment of their peoples, rather than purely monetary returns. Only part of the social returns from such investment will accrue to the governments as monetary flows, and only part, if any, of such flows will be in foreign exchange. Thus, although an aid-financed project may have substantial social returns, there is no necessary link between such returns and the government's ability to find the foreign exchange required to service and repay the aid loans. It is not necessary for the government to have wasted aid for it to find itself encumbered with debt-service problems. Indeed, governments would be irresponsible if, simply in order to insure their future ability to repay loans, they insisted on investing borrowed funds in foreign-exchange-generating projects when such projects were considered to have low social priority.

Implicit in the fiscal responsibility objection is the notion that donors can exert more control over recipients' policies if aid takes the form of loans rather than grants. Ignoring for now (it is taken up in the next chapter), the question of whether or not donors *should* attempt to influence recipients' policies, there is no evidence to support the notion that borrowers are more amenable to persuasion than grantees are. In fact, it is more likely that the opposite claim comes closer to the truth, i.e. that recipients of grants are more likely to be willing to listen to the advice of donors than are borrowers who know that eventually donors will insist on the repayment of their loans, regardless of the purpose for which they were used.

Arguments from pro-aid sources for a higher proportion of

loans in total aid flows have to be taken more seriously. There are two such arguments, both of which claim that the greater the proportion of loans, then the greater will the total aid flow be. The first argues that as the majority of the public in donor countries are basically against aid, it is easier to justify larger aid programs to them if it can be shown that resources are not being given away but only loaned. The second argument is that if the loan element in total aid flows were increased, then as the new loans were repaid, or interest paid on them, this increase in reverse flows could be added to current aid flows and thus the total aid "fund" would be increased.

The first argument is based on the delusion that the public of the rich countries are aware of the composition of their countries' aid programs. In fact, most of the population of most rich countries are only just aware that an aid program exists at all, and most are convinced that all aid is in grant form. Virtually none of the governments of the rich countries have ever made any serious attempt to educate their people about the nature and purpose of their aid programs. To the extent that voters are aware of the overall size of their country's aid program and currently believe that it is all in grant form, they are unlikely to increase their opposition to it if the same annual resource flow was maintained, but all of it was actually given in grant form. No political party (or individual politician) in any developed country has ever tried to substantially enhance its political support by advocating an increased aid program. Indeed, as was noted in Chapter 4, aid programs are unlikely to be included in political platforms at all. In the absence of such leadership it is unlikely that *net* aid flows could be increased by telling voters that aid is to be loaned rather than given away. A pragmatic supporter of aid is probably best advised at present to seek ways in which to increase the net aid content of existing budgetary allocations to aid programs, in particular by pressing for increases in the grant content.

The second argument, that interest payments and amortization flows resulting from the increased lending could be added to the total of new flows, is also based on a delusion. It assumes that present reverse flows (interest and capital repayments) are already added to new aid allocations. Generally, this is not true in most donor countries' programs. Reverse flows simply revert to the treasury as "income." If *all* reverse flows were to be added to new flows, then there would indeed be a continual increase in total *gross* aid flows as repayments and interest accrued. Unless, however, net *new* aid increased even more rapidly, *total net* aid would progressively diminish as the loan proportion increased.

An increase in the loan element of total aid will only increase the size of the total net aid flow if the absolute amount of the new loans has a discounted present value greater than the amount of aid in grant form it replaces. Thus, if a donor wished to replace grants of $100 million with loans for thirty years at 4 percent interest with no grace period, then, using a discount rate of 5 percent, it would have to mount a program of loans valued at $1,042 million in order to equate the real cost to it of the loans with the grants previously provided. (See Chapter 2 for a description of the method of calculating the grant equivalent of loans.)

Given that current levels of gross aid are unlikely to be significantly increased in the foreseeable future, the only possible, sensible way to increase net flows of aid to the Third World is to raise the proportion of gross aid which takes the form of outright gifts. Moreover, some way is going to have to be found, in the not-too-distant future, to lessen the interest and repayment burden placed on less-developed countries by the aid loans of the past.

Subsidized Private Investment

There are, basically, three ways in which governments of the developed countries can encourage, by subsidy, investment in poor countries by domestic companies. First, they can guarantee such investments against some of the "noncommercial" risks which potential investors believe to be present in poor countries. Second, they can tax repatriated profits and interest earned on such investment at preferential rates. And third, they can make capital funds available on concessionary terms for such investment. All three methods are currently being used, and all three can, in theory, raise the flow of private investment funds to less-developed countries, though by how much is a moot point. Some critics argue that such practices simply add to the profits and security of investment which would have taken place anyway.

The subject of private foreign investment in less-developed countries is the source of so much emotionally charged controversy that we should be absolutely clear that here we are only concerned with that part of it which would not have occurred if it had not been for the expenditure of public funds in the rich countries. This should be clear from the definition of aid—the subject matter of this book—as *concessionary* flows of resources. From the point of view of the less-developed countries, it matters little whether any given investment would not have occurred had it not been for a subsidy from the investor's government. The less-developed countries will judge such investments by the same criteria they use for all private foreign investment. The crucial question is whether the developed countries could allocate the resources used up on subsidies in a manner more beneficial to less-developed countries. (Note that these resources will not always figure in aid budgets as to some extent they occur only as income foregone.)

There is no question but that private foreign investment can make a positive contribution to the development of poor countries. It can induce flows of capital and specialized knowledge and skills and provide an entrée into international markets. It can also serve an educational function for workers in the poor countries and generate important economic links with their domestic industry. We can presume that firms which invest in less-developed countries on the basis of commercial decisions, and which meet any terms set by the host governments, are serving a useful purpose. Host governments, as sovereign powers, can *in theory* set any terms they wish as conditions for allowing foreign investors to establish enterprises in their territories. They can change such terms at will to suit changing political and economic circumstances, and they have the ultimate sanction of expropriation. In practice, however, governments of underdeveloped countries are sometimes prevented from setting whatever terms of establishment they wish or from expropriating foreign enterprises out of fear of retaliation from the governments of developed countries or even from some of the large international business concerns. Assuming, as we normally have to, that governments reflect the wishes of their peoples, then a situation in which acceptance by poor countries of the continued operation of foreign enterprises in their territories because of threats made to them must be counted as a worsening of welfare in those countries.

Although the existence of threats of retaliatory action consequent upon expropriation only come to the public notice when actually implemented, the existence of such a threat structure is well known. Any investment which takes place in developing countries as a result of the companies knowing that their governments will "insure" them against expropriation risks with threats of military, diplomatic, or economic action can be considered as unambiguously contrary to the interests of the country invested in. Financial insurance against noncommercial risks provided by the governments of the investing countries can be regarded, in principle, as beneficial to the less-developed countries, and compensation paid out under such schemes can be regarded as aid. In practice, however, we have little experience of such schemes and that which we have suggests that they are likely to be simply grafted on to the threat structure. For example, in 1971, when the democratically elected Marxist government of Chile nationalized the U.S. owned copper mines, it seemed as though the first major call on the resources of the institution operating the U.S. insurance scheme—the Overseas Private Investment Corporation (OPIC)—would result. The compensation which the Chilean government seemed likely to offer was less than the amount that the copper companies had convinced the U.S. government was reasonable, the total resources of OPIC being only a fraction of this sum. Although legally committed to meet the deficit eventually, the United States began to impose economic sanctions on Chile in an attempt to raise the amount of compensation paid by Chile. In such cases the insurance method cannot be regarded as aid or as beneficial to the less-developed countries.

If threat structures lie behind the second and third methods of subsidizing private investment in less-developed countries, they, too, cannot be counted as aid. All they do in that case is lower the cost to domestic interests in the developed countries of engaging in economic activities in the poor countries. Coercion is not aid; rather, it is unacceptable involvement in the affairs of economically and militarily weaker countries. To be sure, some subsidized investment does occur which is not dependent on or supported by the power of the investor's government. Where such investment is acceptable to the people of the countries invested in, it must be counted as beneficial; and the resources the developed countries' governments use up or forego in extending the subsidies should be counted as aid. Note that I wrote "acceptable to the people." There is no doubt that some investment takes place as a result of investing companies taking advantage of the weaknesses of officials and politicians who allow the resources of their countries to be exploited in return for personal gain. "Kickbacks" must be counted as a fact of life in the Third World as well as in the developed countries.

I have not gone into detailed description of the operation of the three mechanisms for encouraging increased flows of private capital to less-developed countries. My concern has been to show, first, that commercially induced flows must be differentiated from those dependent on government subsidies and power, and second, that so-called aid-induced flows may not help the poor countries to improve their lot at all. No other useful generalizations are possible in this context. Each less-developed country has to assess every proposed private foreign investment—purely commercial and aid-induced—in its country according to its needs, its ideologies, and its position in the international structure of intergovernmental relationships. Much, if not most, of the writings of critics and supporters of private foreign investment in less-developed countries is simply the forceful expression of an ideologically based bias supported by selective evidence.

Project versus Program Aid

A dichotomy which illustrates the two basic issues underlying most controversies over the best ways of channeling aid is that of whether aid should be used to finance specific projects which meet specified criteria set by donors or to finance overall development programs. Protagonists on both sides claim that their approach insures maximum efficiency and, depending on their bias, least or most leverage over recipient policies. Both sides are correct on their own terms, and both sides include groups who have different terms or objectives. Both sides, for example, include groups who believe that their approach minimizes involvement in the internal affairs of recipients, which they hold to be desirable, and groups who believe that their approach maximizes involvement, which *they* believe to be desirable.

The involvement, or leverage, issue is discussed in more detail in the next chapter, but it is impossible to discuss the project-program controversy without looking at it in broad outline. Simply put, there are two reasons why donors might feel that they should be involved in the affairs of recipients. First, they might feel that they know what is in the best interests of the recipients who, by implication, do not. Second, donor governments may wish to be able to demonstrate to their taxpayers that the tax-financed aid program is being operated in their interests and/or efficiently. It is, in principle, *easier* to meet both the paternalistic and electoral support motives with an aid program which is predominantly project oriented. This is because aid flows can then be clearly related to specific developments which (hopefully) meet clearly identified criteria. These criteria can take many forms, from simply favoring whole sectors such as agriculture, to highly sophisticated social benefit/cost analyses. Whatever form they take, a project and its performance can, with adequate donor involvement and supervision, be measured against an obvious yardstick.

Critics of the project approach argue that donor agencies never know precisely which project they are financing. It might be, they argue, that while they are financing project *A*, which has the highest priority in the plans of the recipient, the recipient may be using its own funds (no longer required to finance *A*) to finance project *B*. This may be a project which the donors would never have considered for financing. In that case, the critics say, the donor is really financing project *B*. While the paternalistic motive loses some of its validity in the face of this criticism, the electoral support argument stands intact.

Paternalistic donors believe that they know which projects are in the best interests of the recipients and that they are better equipped to supervise their implementation, and maybe even operation. So even if the recipient "wastes" some of its resources in the eyes of donor agencies, they can at least insure that some progress is being made by implementing project *A* efficiently. In fact, the progress actually gained will be equal to that achieved by project *B* plus the extra efficiency with which *A* is carried out. Another paternalist's response to the criticism that recipients can substitute different projects is the claim that by disciplining agencies in the recipient countries to learn and appreciate project evaluation and implementation techniques, they promote the application of more rational criteria to recipients' self-financed projects.

Those who support project lending for electoral reasons are unmoved by criticisms that they are really financing something else. They wish to have aid "showpieces" to hold up so their electorate can see that (at least some) aid is being used in a way it can approve of. They can argue that their taxpayers' money was responsible for whatever hospital, dam, road, harbor, and so forth it paid for directly and ignore, justifiably in view of their motive, sophisticated arguments that they did not really pay for them at all. Moreover, it is always open to the donor agency to argue that it has chosen projects which the recipient governments would not have chosen, and nobody can contradict it. It is a question of who identifies the need for a project in the first instance and the criteria on which the identification is based. Donor *governments* (or executive officers of international agencies) and recipient *governments* may view the same problem with different degrees of concern. Thus a donor government may be concerned with economic and social conditions in a given region of the recipient country whose own government is not. The recipient government may see the acceptance of aid for projects in that region as a price to be paid in order to get other aid or as a net addition to total aid which it would not otherwise get. In either case aid can justifiably be identified with given projects.

At the opposite extreme from paternalistic and electoral support motives for aid—that is, those which lead to support for a project approach—are what might be called, on the one hand the isolationist, and on the other, the anti-imperialism positions, both of which lead to support for a program approach. Supporters of both program-oriented positions argue that the project approach necessarily involves donor governments in the internal affairs of recipient countries. And that is all that the two groups have in common.

Extremist anti-imperialists would argue for the total abolition of aid. Most anti-imperialists, however, would settle for all aid being given as support for overall development programs. They see aid as compensation for past and present exploitation of the poor countries' resources by donor countries, and they assert that the donor countries have no right to attempt to control the poor countries' use of such compensation. This group is not at all concerned with insuring that the recipients use the aid funds efficiently. They see the funds as belonging to the recipients and, consequently, do not believe that the donors have any right to dictate how they will be used. This contrasts with the isolationists' viewpoint. They see a foreign policy role for aid but wish to minimize their own country's involvement in the affairs of the recipient, while insisting that the use of aid funds be subject to surveillance of some sort in order to insure that they are used efficiently. Their basic position derives from a fear that the project approach necessarily involves their nationals in the internal affairs of the recipients in their roles of advisers and technicians. These advisers and technicians are seen in recipients' eyes as representatives of their governments and, as their function is to persuade, to the extent that their persuasion is disliked, antidonor sentiments are created in the recipients. Even worse, if the persuasion is accepted the donors become responsible for the actions taken and so become more involved. They then have a vested interest in insuring the success of the policies, projects, or measures advised upon and will, through their "men on the spot," react negatively against any developments (including political ones) which threaten their success. Some isolationists argue that many of the military involvements of developed countries in less-developed countries since World War II have arisen from such prior economic involvement. While the position of anti-imperialists is fairly clear-cut and justifies general transfers of aid not tied to projects, that of the isolationists who, nevertheless, accept the case (on any grounds) for aid is not. Bilateral and even multilateral program aid is actually likely to mean even greater involvement in the internal affairs of recipients than is required by a project approach. The U.S. Agency for International Development proposals for the 1972 economic assistance program submitted to Congress in the spring of 1971 said this about program aid:

> [U.S.] program loans help to avoid or to minimize government controls which might otherwise be necessary. The loan funds and the commodities to be imported may be designed to support the

introduction of specific policies and measures agreed by the recipient, usually with one of the international agencies. The loans are made on the understanding that such self-help measures to improve the performance of the economy are actually enacted. Such measures might include adopting more realistic or flexible exchange rates, removing or reducing restrictions on imports, providing incentives to exports, increasing revenues through new or increased taxation or better tax administration, limiting the size of the money supply, and undertaking land reform and other institutional changes essential to development.

This is tantamount to saying that the United States insists that recipients forego sovereignty over a substantial part of their economic and social policy and meet standards of performance set by U.S. officials in order to continue to receive U.S. program aid. No project approach supporter ever desired so much power! It is easy to see why so many isolationists have become disenchanted with a bilaterally run program approach to aid. And, as we will see in the next chapter, channeling of aid funds through international agencies does not guarantee freedom from such involvement.

Both the project and program approaches to aid can involve donors in the internal affairs of the recipients. Whether or not they do depends on the extent to which donors are concerned with seeing that the aid funds they provide are used by the recipients in a way which the donors consider to be progressive and efficient. Only the approach of the anti-imperialists offers any serious scope for donors to disengage themselves from the internal affairs of recipients. To do so successfully, however, requires that donors give complete control over aid funds to recipients and remove decisions on amounts of aid and its distribution from the political arenas in their own countries. In fact, it is not possible to remove aid from the political arena in donor countries while taxpayers' money is involved and while their governments seek to justify the allocation and use of aid in terms of what it buys.[1] Several proposals have been

---

[1] See Chapters 3 and 4 for a discussion of this point.

made for breaking the link between aid flows and taxpayers in donor countries. They do not, however, escape from the issue of control, nor can they while what is essentially involved is a transfer of resources from rich to poor countries. Even an anti-imperialistic program with no taxpayer link cannot escape from the politics of allocation of aid among contending recipients as long as total aid funds available are less than total recipient demand for them.

Compensatory and Supplementary Finance Schemes

Many observers argue that apart from needing aid to supplement the domestic resources available to support their development programs, the less-developed countries need to be able to count on smoothly continuous flows of foreign exchange to pay for the imports which are essential to those programs. They argue that violent year-to-year fluctuations in foreign exchange receipts seriously hamper the efficient implementation of development plans. Some of the logic of the case made for commodity agreements derives from these beliefs; proponents argue that because many less-developed countries are more or less dependent on exports of a few primary products whose prices fluctuate markedly on world markets, intervention in those markets to stabilize prices would allow such countries to plan their development with more confidence. However, just as the difficulties of such arrangements prevent their being effectively used to increase the flow of resources (as we shall see in the next section), so do they seriously limit the possibility of stabilizing that flow. Arising from the disappointments with international commodity agreements were proposals for financial schemes to insure the development programs of less-developed countries against the problems which might result from unexpected fluctuations in their foreign exchange earnings.

To meet a somewhat different purpose the International Monetary Fund (IMF) has been operating a Compensatory Finance Scheme since 1963 (the original scheme was expanded and its scope widened slightly in 1966). This scheme is definitely not intended as a vehicle for the transfer of resources from rich to poor countries. It is aimed simply at providing temporary balance-of-payments relief to countries who are suffering from what are considered *by the IMF* to be short-run unexpected shortfalls in export proceeds. Any funds loaned under this scheme must be repaid over a fairly short period (two to five years) and cannot be regarded as aid in the sense understood here.

At the 1964 UNCTAD a proposal was made for Supplementary Financial Measures (SFM) which would use genuine aid to achieve longer run compensation for shortfalls in export proceeds. As we have already seen, whenever a claim is made that aid is needed for some specific purpose, we have the problem of determining how much is needed. In this case it would seem, on the face of it, that such an estimate would be relatively easy. All we need to know is the difference in any year between the foreign exchange *requirements* of the development plan and actual *receipts*. Unfortunately, it has proved so difficult to agree on a method of calculating this difference that little progress has been made on the Supplementary Financial Measures proposal. The reader who recalls Chapter 5 can guess why: while it is easy to count how much foreign exchange flows into a country over a given period, it is impossible to determine "requirements" unequivocally. In this proposal, however, agreement would have to be reached between each less-developed country and the agency operating the scheme on the actual level of the "reasonable expectations" of foreign exchange earnings on which the country's development program was planned. And as the scheme would obviously take into account only those shortfalls of foreign exchange earnings which were beyond the country's control, there is obviously considerable scope for disagreement over what factors are "beyond control."

Even if politically neutral statistical rules for the distribution of supplementary finance could be agreed on, the scheme has not been supported (to any meaningful extent) by the donor countries or even by many potential recipients. From the donors' point of view the high degree of automaticity in the proposed SFM and its multilateral basis reduce the possibility both of politically determined aid distribution and of bilateral leverage over the policies of individual recipients. The recipients' view will depend on the extent to which funds allocated by donors to the scheme are net additions to their total subventions. If it only represents a shift in the mechanism for the distribution of existing aid levels then some recipient countries, those who do not expect shortfalls in export earnings, will be hostile to the scheme, as it will probably reduce their share of total aid flows. They may be hostile, too, if the agency chosen to administer the SFM were to be given powers to exclude from participation in the scheme countries whose development plans are not considered "realistic" or whose claims concerning expected export receipts are regarded as overoptimistic.

The proposed scheme for SFM can be faulted on technical grounds, too. In the first place, as has been stressed earlier, there is no obvious correlation between the need for aid shown by a country and its balance-of-payments situation. Second, the scheme would create incentives for individual countries to distort their growth pattern in favor of inefficient import-substitution industries in that having a guarantee of minimum foreign exchange receipts, they would increase their total aid receipts by diverting resources from export activities to import-substitution activities. Third, as the scheme would operate in terms of periods, incentives would be created for poor countries to create at the end of the period situations which were seemingly beyond their control (dock strikes, for example). These would reduce total export receipts in the accounting period. Fourth, it would create incentives for corrupt practices to emerge, ranging from underinvoicing of exports to outright manipulation of trade data. Finally, and perhaps most seriously, it would create incentives for gearing domestic policies toward maximizing benefits under the scheme rather than the efficient attainment of domestic objectives.

Control of Primary Product Markets

Various schemes have been proposed for interfering in markets for primary products in ways designed to increase the transfer of resources from consumers to producers. Although the detailed mechanisms of the schemes vary, they all have the common elements of devices designed to increase the income received by the producers, mostly by increasing prices of the products. Some are specifically designed to reduce the supplies entering markets and so raise prices; examples of this type are the existing arrangements for tin and tea. Others work by reducing the quantities consumers can afford by directly raising the price they have to pay; examples are the arrangements concerning the U.K. coal market, the U.S. sugar market, and those covering most of the world's oil market. Probably the bulk of such schemes operate within and among the developed countries and are designed as domestic measures to redistribute incomes among the citizens of those countries. Two, however, the International Coffee and Tea Agreements, were established specifically to transfer resources (by raising prices for reduced supplies) from rich, consuming nations to poor, producing countries. Other schemes, including one for cocoa with a similar objective, are currently being negotiated.

Although such schemes may have desirable subsidiary purposes (such as price stabilization) and although they may be applauded if they involve transfers of resources to poor countries resulting from the counterbalancing of monopolistic trade practices in rich countries, they cannot be advocated as a major means of channeling aid to less-developed countries. This is because the transfers involved are purely arbitrary and bear no relation to the needs of individual, less-developed countries for foreign exchange. In effect, they represent a tax on consumers of the individual commodities, the proceeds of which tend to be used to subsidize the incomes of the owners (who may not need such assistance) of the resources used to produce them. It may be argued that the governments of producing countries can impose taxes designed to cream off such benefits in the producing countries. The producers of the commodities, however, frequently constitute a powerful lobby for the prevention of the imposition of such taxes. If a commodity is of sufficient importance to the economy, such a lobby may, in fact, be the most powerful part of the government and, as such, unlikely to advocate taxes on itself. The result may be, and often is, that relatively poor consumers in rich countries are "taxed" in order to subsidize the rich producers in poor countries, which does not give much force to the argument that commodity agreements can provide development resources for the Third World. Why should rich countries allocate their aid according to their import pattern for specific commodities? Aid should be allocated among poor countries according to those criteria for distribution which have proved politically acceptable in donor countries or in multilateral agencies for distribution according to internationally accepted criteria. Finally, it is clear that if donors wish to control the use of aid flows, it will be virtually impossible to do so if such aid is transferred via trade channels, as it is usually impossible to identify and siphon off that element of the trade payments which represents aid. Even if it were possible to identify it, attempts by donors to persuade the governments of producing countries to divert what appears in the records as producers' incomes would be regarded as totally unacceptable interference in domestic affairs. Imagine the furor there would be in the United States if the Indian government attempted to persuade Congress to tax that part of the income of U.S. farmers which results from sales of wheat to India and allocate the proceeds to, say, urban renewal programs!

Even if all the difficulties were to be overcome and prices effectively raised and total resource flows increased, it should be borne in mind that every increase in prices will, in the long run, reduce the value of such trade if consumers switch their demand to cheaper substitutes. In addition, while artificially high prices are maintained in some lines of production, resources will be attracted into them, possibly away from alternative employment in which they were used more efficiently.

Experience in negotiating for and the operation of such schemes has shown us that where several competing producing countries are involved, it usually proves impossible to agree on how the market should be interfered with in order to produce the extra resource flow. (This difficulty is not confined to less-developed country producers; it arises in many such negotiations and schemes among developed countries.) Different forms of intervention will benefit (or harm) different producers in different ways, and, obviously, each is out for the most he can get. Clearly, compromise is essential if such schemes are to operate at all, and compromise agreements in the sphere of international trade are probably the most difficult of all agreements to reach. Negotiations for an International Cocoa Agreement lasted for more than a decade before a scheme was finally agreed on (even now it has not been ratified by all participants and the major consumer—the United States—has not accepted it). Similarly, the Coffee Agreement collapsed in 1972 due to squabbles among the producing countries, and between them as a group and the importing countries.

The Liquidity Link

It will not have escaped the reader's attention that international monetary relations have been the subject of much controversy in recent years. Many proposals for their reform have been put forward. Among the criticisms of the existing arrangements has been the assertion that they do not take sufficiently into account the problems and needs of the less-developed countries. And among the proposals for reform have been suggestions that any new arrangements instituted should include a link between plans for the expansion of the means of settling international debts—i.e. liquidity—and the provision of aid to poor countries by rich countries. There are several versions of the link proposal, but they are all derived from the same basic idea. This is, that whatever new instrument is decided on as the internationally accepted method of payment for international debts (incurred by buying goods or services or by borrowing money, for example), its initial distribution should be biased, maybe completely, in favor of the less-developed countries. A brief historical account of the international payments mechanism may help to clarify this complex issue. Until the crisis of 1971 the world had, since World War II, operated an international payments mechanism known as the "gold exchange" standard. In theory, this meant that all international debts could be settled with either gold or currency. In practice, only those currencies which were regarded as having fixed long-term value in terms of gold were accepted as settlement of debts. This meant that the supply of international liquidity was geared to the world production of gold and to continual payments deficits maintained by those countries in whose currencies the world community had confidence. The only two currencies which the world, for a long time, regarded as strong—i.e. stable in terms of their gold value—were the dollar and sterling. Thus, if the international payments system required more liquidity than could be met by the production of gold, it had to allow the United States and the United Kingdom to run payments deficits. Effectively, then, while the United States and the United Kingdom could pay their international debts in either gold or their own currency, other countries had either to earn dollars or sterling in some way or to pay debts in gold, if they had any. The postwar growth in trade was so rapid that with gold production rising only slowly great demand built up for dollars and sterling, with the main emphasis on dollars as the war and its aftermath had reduced confidence in the long-term stability of the pound. The whole situation was inherently unstable, however, for as the United States ran continual balance-of-payments deficits which accumulated over time, confidence in the long-run value of the dollar in terms of gold and other currencies began to sag.

Awareness of the need to develop new methods for settling international debts independent of the productivity of gold mines and of the state of key economies expanded slowly. It was increasingly agreed that any new payments instrument would have to be geared to the needs of the payments system and nothing else. A decision to create a new payments instrument was taken in 1968, and it came into existence in 1969 as Special Drawing Rights (SDRs) on the International Monetary Fund (IMF). Once the decision to *create* a new international means of payment had been taken, the problem obviously arose of how to distribute it among participants in the scheme. This was solved, initially at least, by allocating SDRs to countries in (more or less) proportion to their basic quotas in the IMF; these quotas, in turn, being determined with respect to the economic size of the member. Advocates of the aid-liquidity link argued that they should have been distributed according to the *needs* of the economies for international purchasing power, with most or all being allocated in the first instance to less-developed countries.

The aid-liquidity link proposal is very much a "two birds with one stone" idea. On the one hand, the proposers argue, the less-developed countries are desperately short of the international purchasing power they need to finance their development programs. On the other hand, the whole world trading community needs to insure an adequate flow of international means of payment—i.e. international purchasing power. Why not contribute to the solution of both problems, they ask, by distributing the newly created international purchasing power to the poor countries in the first instance? The poor countries, they hold, are unlikely to hoard the new means of payment but are likely to put it into circulation immediately by increasing their purchases of imports. Various possible mechanisms have been suggested for the actual operation of the schemes. They need not concern us here. There is no doubt that such a scheme would provide a source of aid for poor countries and that it could provide for the liquidity requirements of the trading community. But even though it would provide a means of escaping some of the political problems of existing forms of aid, such a scheme is most unlikely to be implemented in the foreseeable future because it would introduce new and even less acceptable problems.

Critics of the link proposal point out that while bilateral involvement would be reduced (which makes it unacceptable to those who believe there *should* be bilateral involvement), multilateral involvement would increase, because international agencies would be supervising a greater proportion of total aid. The liquidity-creating institution or its agent would have to decide on the allocation of the new liquidity among the poor countries; and critics argue that decisions on the allocation of aid should be exercised by a competent aid agency rather than one whose prime function should be the supervision of the international monetary mechanism. Other critics argue that using SDRs to provide aid removes any control donors (individually or collectively) have or would like to have over the use of aid: recipients of SDRs are free to spend them on whatever they want. Finally, if developed countries reduce their explicit aid subventions directly in proportion to the aid they would be implicitly called upon to extend via the link schemes, then nothing would have been gained in terms of total resource flows. These, and other, criticisms of the link proposals are simply pointing out the difficulties involved in attempting to kill two birds with one stone; it is possible, but it would demand a degree of political willingness to operate the scheme which is not likely to emerge in international relations in the foreseeable future.

Any successful attempt to ameliorate those difficulties of the international monetary mechanism which stem from inadequate supplies of acceptable international liquidity will help to remove existing domestic political criticism of aid programs on grounds of balance-of-payments problems. Thus, many observers feel that it is best to concentrate on seeking the most efficient solution to the liquidity problem, rather than constraining the choice of solution to one, including an aid link, which would be most unlikely to result in an increase in net aid. They also feel that future flows of aid should not be made conditional on the need of the international monetary mechanism for new injections of liquidity.

Technical Assistance

In his 1970 annual report to the DAC, its chairman wrote:

> The vital role of technical assistance has been increasingly recognized by all donors during the sixties, both as a condition of the efficient utilization of capital aid and as an essential contribution towards human development in the recipient countries.

He added, however,

> The record of the sixties (on such key issues as the quality of technical assistance supplied, its adaptation to the needs of the recipients and to their development priorities, its coordination with other forms of aid and among the various suppliers) has left much to be desired.[2]

It cannot be denied that there is much technical knowledge in developed countries which can be used to help achieve the desired transformation and modernization of poor countries. The transfer of such knowledge must, however, be effected on a personal basis, bringing individual people face-to-face at the forefront of the rich-poor aid relationship. Such confrontations necessarily involve political considerations. A two-way flow of people is involved: first of experts and advisers to less-developed countries and second of personnel from those countries to the developed countries for training or study. The purpose of such movements is persuasion: persuasion by experts and advisers of their counterparts in poor countries of the efficacy of specific policies or practices and persuasion of students and trainees as to the value of certain modes of analysis and prac-

[2] Report by Chairman Edwin M. Martin. *1970 Review, Development Assistance* (Paris: OECD, 1970), page 59.

tices. In this latter case, at least, we should not shy away from the word "indoctrination." At the root of technical assistance is obviously the notion that "rich countries know best."

Technical assistance of the first type covers all manner of subjects, from ideal syllabuses for primary school children to optimum population policies, from electoral reform to military strategy, and from efficient customs organization to optimum exchange rate policies. While some such attempts at persuasion may seem politically innocuous, as in the case of the ideal layout of a factory, others are based on value judgments derived from specific sociopolitical environments and obviously run the risk of culture clashes. For example, while it is one thing to receive through the mail a pamphlet advocating certain sorts of government responsibility to and for the private sector of industry and/or foreign investors, it is quite another matter to have a foreigner sitting in your office trying to convince you of the usefulness of his or her government's (or even some international committee's) views. If the official believes that future flows of aid to his country may depend on the adviser's report on his reaction to the "advice" proffered, he is confronted with a serious dilemma. Clearly the intellectual or cultural arrogance which characterizes such confrontations tends to lead to a dominance-dependence relationship, even if the persuader's motives are politically pure. Many (not all) advisers from rich countries and international institutions, being human, tend to "grade" the governments of the countries they advise as wise or stupid, amenable or perverse, enlightened or misguided, according to the extent to which their advice is accepted and acted on. At a lower level of political involvement a similar attitude is found in rich countries toward the trainees and students from less-developed countries.

If the recipient government accepts and acts on the advice offered to it, then the advisers are morally responsible for the outcome. In practice, they are not held actually responsible because the government could have, in theory, refused to accept and act on the advice. There are many examples, however, where the dominance-dependence relationship was so strong that the recipient was effectively obliged to accept and act on the advice given to it by representatives, even when the resultant policies were politically repugnant to the recipient. If the policies fail, as they frequently do, it is the recipient government which is held responsible by its citizens for their failures. Citizens of dependent countries have no way of attaching responsibility to the donor institutions, although they may generate ill-feeling toward them. Failures of such policies may occur for many reasons: foreign advisers may incorrectly assess the social and political aspirations of the countries they advise; their understanding of the workings of the economic structure of the countries may be wrong; and/or the theoretical basis of their advice may be unsound. Whatever the reason, the costs of the failure are borne by the poor country. Unless donors are prepared to underwrite such costs, they should not assume, as many of their representatives do, that they have a monopoly of wisdom.

Apart from the probability that advice may be wrong, there are other problems with technical assistance. Obviously, the presence of a team of visibly rich advisers and the sight of the resources made available for them (e.g. grand hotels and expensive cars) in a country characterized by extreme poverty can and does lead to resentment and unrest. Shouts of "Yankee go home" and "Gringo" come from the heart. The presence of rich, well-fed, healthy advisers flown in for a brief period and surrounded by luxury to, say, advise peasants living at subsistence level on how to farm, must lead to bitterness and potential conflict. The white man not only took physical disease to poor countries, but also spread the seeds of discontent.

Another problem arises when the advisers come on a bilateral, country-to-country basis. If a government relies heavily on teams from one donor country, then in the eyes of its citizens—and other countries—it is seen to be politically involved with that donor. Any political feelings which the citizens (and other countries) have toward the donor involved will tend to be felt and magnified toward the recipient government. Even if the advice is correct and useful, the government may be regarded as politically tainted and lose support. There are also problems associated with students from poor countries studying and training in donor countries. They may be taught by people who have no knowledge (or worse, biased or wrong knowledge) of conditions in the student's country, and, consequently, the students may learn skills, techniques, and modes of analysis which, at best, are irrelevant to their country's needs. They may be affected by life styles in their host country which may alienate and isolate them when they return home; indeed, they may not (and frequently do not) return home.

International Taxes

Much thought has been given in recent years to devising forms of aid which would be free from some of the political difficulties and inefficiencies of existing mechanisms. One version of the proposal which has been made is that a tax be charged on the use of some non-nationally owned resource (examples which have been suggested are sea-bed resources and the seas and air for transport), and the proceeds paid into a fund for distribution to the poor countries of the world. The merits of such proposals are that they would remove the political difficulties and inherent uncertainty involved in deciding on annual national budgetary allocations for aid purposes. They would also remove the possibility of bilateral leverage which is justified in terms of insuring the efficient use of citizens' tax money. The reader will see that this proposal for an international tax is similar in nature to the aid-liquidity link proposal and, as such, subject to the same sort of doubts and criticisms.

The first problem is that once the world community, or some subgroup of it, decided to create property rights in non-nationally owned natural resources, most nations would seek to influence control over the distribution of such rights. It is inconceivable, given the present state of international relations, that all developed countries would agree to forego all rights in the resources and would not in varying degrees demand "their share." Just as their willingness to provide aid to less-developed countries varies considerably now, so would their willingness to pay taxes on their use of what they considered "their share" of, say, the sea bed or, for that matter, on anybody else's share. Second, even if such chauvinism could be overcome, the problems of determining the distribution of the tax proceeds would remain, with all the attendant problems of assessing needs and criteria for use. Under this scheme all less-developed countries would be encouraged to feel that they had a right to a share in the proceeds, and interstate jealousies and rivalries would lead to continuous dispute over the "correct" allocation. Most existing donor agencies deal with member countries—rich and poor—on a bilateral basis. In the tax scheme, however, the agency would have to deal with rich countries as a group (as suppliers of the resources the tax proceeds would mostly be spent on) and with the recipients as a group to determine the allocation. Such an international scheme would depend for its success on a degree of international goodwill, reflected in willingness to compromise, which has never yet been achieved in international relations.

Apart from being politically utopian, the scheme is inherently inefficient. First, it would involve a complicated and expensive administrative structure to monitor its operation and to prevent evasion. Second, to the extent that taxes were paid, relative prices would be altered in such a way as to discourage use of the resource taxed. And third, less obviously, by discriminately placing the burden of the tax only on consumers of products incorporating the taxed resources (e.g. air travel), the scheme would tend to raise the welfare cost of accumulating a given amount of revenue.

Conclusion

Anyone who is generally in favor of resources being transferred from developed to less-developed countries will be tempted to applaud any scheme which holds out a promise of adding to that flow and will also tend to underplay the difficulties involved in such schemes. Similarly, any critic of aid in general will tend to point out and stress the difficulties associated with all schemes. Dissatisfaction with existing levels or forms of aid inspire observers of the aid process continually to devise new ways of raising levels or improving the form it takes. There is no ideal solution, and there cannot be. There can be no agreement on the optimum level of aid while there is no agreement over its purpose, and, similarly, there can be no one ideal form for aid while it is serving several, sometimes conflicting, purposes. It happens from time to time, however, that broad agreement does seem to be reached on far-reaching changes in the overall structures of the aid process. For example, a consensus appears to be emerging that an increasing proportion of aid flows should be channeled through international agencies. This issue is taken up in the next chapter.

VII

THE MULTILATERAL / BILATERAL
DEBATE

The ultimate source of all aid funds is the taxpayers in the rich countries. They like their governments to assure them occasionally that such funds are being used wisely and effectively. As we have seen, however, in several places in this book, there is no agreement on a common definition of what constitutes wisdom. Nor is there any consensus as to what institutions or which people can be trusted to insure that aid is used effectively. Even if we confined ourselves to the (unrealistic) assumption that only four homogeneous groups are involved in the aid process—donor country taxpayers, their governments, recipient governments, and their citizens—it would only be by chance that the conception of wisdom and the preferred methods of institutional control of aid of the four groups would coincide. In fact, as we have seen, there are conflicts over what constitutes a "wise" use of aid among donor governments, among taxpayers in donor countries and between them and their governments, between donor and recipient governments, and among recipient governments and between them and various groups of their citizens. There are similar intragroup and intergroup conflicts over the question of which organizations can best be trusted to insure that the aid funds which are available are used effectively.

Should Donors Attempt to Control the Use of Aid?

The conflicts over what constitutes a wise use of aid funds are a natural reflection of the diversity of political viewpoints in the world community. As long as different participants in the aid process hold different views on the uses to which aid should be put, it is only to be expected that supporters of each objective will tend to believe that other objectives are unwise. For example, we saw in Chapter 4 that some U.S. Congressmen believe that U.S. aid should be used to support independent nations in the Third World, while others feel that it should be used to create links of dependency on which the United States could draw to further its own interests. Such differing viewpoints can hardly be reconciled. Similarly, many of those who in 1971 supported the provision of aid to the government of South Vietnam, enabling it to destroy its own economy, environment, and even people, refused to support the right of India to defend its own economy, environment, and people. More traditional conflicts arise between supporters of capitalism and supporters of the various forms of socialism, and between those who believe that donors should decide how aid should be used and those who believe that recipient governments should decide that issue. Many of the controversies within and among donor countries arise out of the prevalent belief held there that aid is either paternalistic charity or motivated by self-interest. Charity is almost always based on the conviction that the charitable know what is best for the recipients of their largesse. Similarly, self-interested aid depends for its existence and continuance on the identification and furthering of self-interest.

Donor agencies and their leaders who control the supply of aid can impose their views on the "correct" use of aid as a condition of its disbursement. While there are no universally accepted criteria of "correctness," this concentration of effective power over the use of aid must inevitably set up tensions between the agencies and those who do not agree with its concept of correctness. The existence of this tension has led to continuous controversy both among those who accept the assumed right of donors to control the use of aid funds and among those who question that right. As attitudes toward aid encompass opinions covering the totality of the economic, social, political, and military conditions of most of the world's inhabitants, an exhaustive analysis of these controversies would be an immense undertaking. Some of these have been touched on elsewhere in the book and others must be left out; this chapter concentrates on the debate surrounding the structure of control over aid-disbursing agencies.

The Radical View

The radical view is that aid should be regarded as compensation for the detrimental effects of the arbitrary economic discrimination which rich countries have been able to impose on poor countries by means of their superior economic or military power. Few people would deny that such discrimination did and does take place in many forms, such as discriminatory trade and shipping arrangements and monopolistic management of many product markets. Colonial empires were established in order to maximize the benefits of such discriminatory practices for the rich imperial powers. Although formal imperialism has almost ended, the discrimination continues. The implication of the argument for providing aid as compensation is, then, that it would be simply a process of transferring resources back to the countries to which they really belong; so those countries should, therefore, be allowed to use them in whatever manner they think fit, even if such use would appear wasteful by donor standards. Much expenditure in rich countries (space exploration, for example) is regarded as frivolous and wasteful by the inhabitants of poor countries, but their views are dismissed by the donors as irrelevant, outside interference. Why, then, should the poor countries listen to the admonitions and advice of donors? The "aid as compensation" lobby argues that the dominance-dependence relationship of the rich and poor countries allows rich countries to impose their economic, social, political, and even military values on poor countries and that this imposition justifies the "neocolonialism" label given to it by its critics.

The "aid as compensation" argument has considerable intellectual appeal to radicals and some liberals. Any specialist in the study of economic relations between rich and poor countries can point to many ways in which the former discriminate against the latter out of self-interest and deprive the poor countries of some of the means of financing their own development. However, the argument points to its own contradiction: just as rich countries exploit poor countries, so do the rich minorities in poor countries exploit their poorer fellow citizens. No one who has traveled through the Third World could argue otherwise. It is very unlikely that, in many less-developed countries, funds provided as compensation would be used by their rich, elitist governments and industrial leaders primarily to ameliorate the distress of the poorer sections of their countries. Even where there is a genuine desire to obtain aid and use it sincerely for the raising of the living standards of the very poor, it does not follow that those in control of the economy will know how best to use the aid for this purpose. Because a man is a citizen or leader of a poor country, he does not necessarily have any greater claim to knowledge of the causes of, or methods of eradicating, poverty. The defect with the "aid as compensation" argument is, then, that its advocates in the developed countries tend to believe that all people in poor countries are qualitatively different—more humane or more intelligent in economic and social matters—than their own fellow countrymen. Their belief that the governments of poor countries can be relied upon to insure an equitable and efficient use of their countries' resources is contradicted by the evidence of increasingly polarized income distribution and economically wasteful investment and consumption in those countries.

The Conservative View

In complete opposition to those who believe that donors should exert no control at all over the use of aid are those who believe that "he who pays the piper calls the tune." The rationale of this conservative viewpoint is derived from the fact that the funds used to finance aid programs have alternative private or public uses in donor countries. This group argues that those in control of donor aid programs should insure that the benefits *donors* derive from spending national resources on aid should at least equal the benefits which could have been obtained by spending them "at home." They feel that the only certain way to insure such an equality is for the donors' agencies to have complete control over the use of aid by recipients.

Control of aid implies to conservatives that donor agencies select the recipients, define the purposes for which aid can be used, and rigorously supervise the projects financed by the aid. Donor control is felt to be required in order to insure that only those recipients who can effectively and efficiently use aid, in ways which are considered beneficial to donors, actually receive the aid which is available. The inevitable involvement in the internal affairs of recipients which such control entails is regarded by conservatives as a price the poor countries must pay in order to receive aid. There is no reason at all why donor agencies and recipient governments should always agree on what constitutes effective and efficient use of aid. When disagreements arise, as they do, tensions are created between those involved. These tensions may be serious if the donor agencies insist, as a condition for aid, that the recipient government follow policies which it does not view with favor. If the recipient government refuses to follow the policies preferred by the donor, either it can refuse to accept aid or the donor can refuse to supply aid. Conservatives see nothing wrong with such confrontation, believing that the right to give or withhold aid is a donor prerogative.

When bilateral donor agencies become involved with the affairs of recipient governments and clashes of opinion occur, the resulting tensions are likely to stir up sentiments of political hostility toward the donor. If the donor government considers it important for its national interests—economic or military—it may use its superior economic or military power in an attempt to force its policies on the recipient government. Such use of force naturally deepens the antagonisms between the donor government and the recipient's government and/or citizens. Among the Western countries only the United States has sufficient economic or military power at its disposal, and the will to use it, to force its views on recipient governments, although other donors have refused aid to poor countries which follow policies out of line with those they favor. Conservatives approve of such actions. They may approve because they believe that donor interests should have priority over recipient interests. Many people in donor countries support the cutting off of aid to, or even military invasion of, poor countries who threaten donor investment in their country or the apparent military security of the donor. The examples of Cuba, Vietnam, Ecuador, (aid for which was cut off by the United States in 1972 due to U.S. concern with fishing rights and U.S. investments in oil exploration there), Spain, and Malta come readily to mind. Even liberals and radicals approve the use of economic force against a poor country when they, too, dislike the policies of the recipient; and here the examples of Egypt, Pakistan (in 1972), and Rhodesia are fresh in the memory.

When involvement in the domestic affairs of poor countries results in vociferous resentment of the donor or in massive injections of finance, many people in donor countries come to resent what they see as the cause of such hostility or expenditure—their bilateral aid program. Those who react, for any reason, against their country's direct involvement in the domestic affairs of poor countries but who support the principle of aid—out of self-interest or for humanitarian reasons—naturally look for ways of continuing to transfer resources from rich to poor countries which do not entail such bilateral involvement. In reacting against bilateral control of aid they come to support an increasing role for multilateral institutions in the aid process. For example, we saw in Chapter 4 how support for multilateral institutions grew in the U.S. Congress during the late 1960s and early 1970s due to the desire, felt by many Congressmen, to move away from bilateral involvement.

A Compromise View: Multilateralism

In addition to those people and politicians in donor countries who have come to support multilateral aid agencies as a result of a distaste for bilateral involvement with recipients, there are others who believe that these agencies should play a more important role in aid transactions for other reasons. There are those, for example, who believe that the control of aid should be removed as far as possible from domestic political issues in donor countries. Idealistic internationalists also welcome any move to increase the importance of the role of multilateral institutions, as do governments of poor countries who wish to move away from dependence on a specific donor or group of donors.

Five (not completely independent) virtues are commonly claimed for aid channeled through multilateral agencies. These are: (1) freedom from prejudiced control by individual donors; (2) removal from the vagaries of domestic political issues in donor countries; (3) increased acceptability to recipients; (4) sound, common, and well-known criteria for its allocation; and (5) efficient supervision.

We have already seen how the distribution and use of aid extended by bilateral donors may be determined by the foreign policies, business interests, and value judgments on the nature of "desirable development" of individual donors. Advocates of multilateralization of aid contend that as multilateral agencies do not have foreign policies or business interests of their own, and that as they include citizens of poor countries among their executive and operational staff members, their methods of control must be politically neutral and concerned only with seeking to help poor countries move efficiently toward an agreed concept of development. The partisans of multilateralism accept that, as the total amount of resources available for aid is limited, some measure of control is necessary in order to insure that it is used as productively as possible. Given the need for some form of control, they argue that this is best exercised by agencies whose sole reason for having been created is to further the cause of development in poor countries.

The second argument used in support of increasing the flow of aid through multilateral agencies is that these agencies, in contrast to the bilateral ones, are not affected in their day-to-day operations by the domestic politics of individual donors. It is clear that bilateral agencies, staffed as they are by the servants of individual governments and answerable directly to those governments, must reflect the policies of their governments if they are to continue in existence. To take an extreme example, no bilateral agency could extend aid to a poor country which aggressively allies itself with countries considered to be enemies of the donor country. At a more common level, if a poor country actively discriminates against the business interests of a donor country, the bilateral aid agency of that donor is likely to be instructed not to extend aid to the poor country in question. Donors' domestic affairs may also affect their bilateral aid programs while leaving their contributions to multilateral agencies unaffected. Thus, when a donor faces a balance-of-payments crisis or unemployment problems at home, it may cut back on the size of its bilateral aid program but maintain its contributions to multilateral agencies in order to satisfy international commitments or simply to save face. Given the basically hostile attitude of taxpayers in most donor countries toward aid, little justification is needed for a reduction in bilateral aid. Reductions in multilateral contributions have to be explained and justified in open international forums. Supporters of aid in general, then, tend to favor multilateralization in order to escape the constraint imposed by domestic politics on bilateral agencies.

Third, recipients are assumed by the multilateralists to prefer multilateral aid to bilateral aid. The grounds for this assumption are that (1) recipients are saved the need to "go the rounds" of individual donors, making a case for contributions from their various bilateral agencies in order to raise the total sum they require; (2) it allows them to escape the need to somehow align their foreign and economic policies with those of donor countries; (3) it removes a possible source of humiliation arising from dependency on specific countries; and (4) it allows them to develop long-term relationships and understandings with neutral specialists who maintain common and consistent criteria for aid use, rather than the donor politicians and officers whose power and influence (and thus the criteria used to control aid) may change from election to election.

Fourth, as already mentioned, instead of many bilateral agencies confronting poor countries with several (changeable) sets of criteria for the distribution and use of aid, each derived from the individual domestic political frameworks of the donors, multilateral agencies can be assumed to use a single set of internationally agreed criteria. With only one set of criteria for the distribution and use of aid, geared toward the single objective of development (as understood by the agencies), poor countries are more likely to achieve their objective than when they are trying to meet several criteria simultaneously, each geared to different objectives (which may simply be the different donors' conceptions of "development").

Finally, multilateralists claim that their favored agencies are more efficient than bilateral agencies. This claim is based on the belief that a small number of large multilateral agencies are more likely to be able to allow their personnel to specialize on countries or subjects (e.g. transport or health), thus gaining more experience and expertise than could a larger number of smaller bilateral agencies, in which the staff may be required to be generalists rather than specialists. A second basis for the claim of superior efficiency (used here in the sense of a lower ratio of administrative cost to the total aid flow) of multilateral agencies is that they are able to save expensive time and scarce resources by not having to discuss and clear their programs with various government departments, as do bilateral agencies.

Whatever the empirical validity of the various claims made in support of increasing the proportion of total aid channeled through multilateral agencies, it is clear that they have over the last decade held some sway in the corridors of power in the donor countries. This is demonstrated by the tripling of the flow of finance controlled by these agencies in that period from around $500 million in 1960 to around $1500 million in 1970, although only two-thirds of those totals can be claimed as "aid" according to the definition being used in this book.

The Multilateral Aid Agencies

Broadly speaking, there are two basic types of multilateral aid agencies. There are those whose prime purpose is the provision of technical assistance to poor countries—the so-called Specialized Agencies of the United Nations. The nature of the specialized technical assistance provided by these agencies is for the most part indicated by their titles: for example, the Food and Agriculture Organization (FAO), the United Nations Industrial Development Organization (UNIDO), the United Nations Educational, Scientific, and Cultural Organization (UNESCO), and the World Health Organization (WHO). The activities of the various agencies are coordinated by the Secretariat of the United Nations Development Program (UNDP).

The second type of multilateral agency is concerned with the provision of capital resources to poor countries. In this class are the various international banks, such as the International Bank for Reconstruction and Development (and its subsidiaries, the International Development Association and the International Finance Corporation), and the Asian, African, and Inter-American Development Banks.

Our attention in this book has been primarily focused on the aid-financed transfer of goods from rich to poor countries rather than with the transfer of services—that is, technical assistance. While there is some two-way overlapping of functions between the two types of agencies, it is primarily the banks which engage in this transfer of goods. And while reference is made to the Specialized Agencies for comparative purposes, the discussion in this and subsequent sections concentrates on the international banks and the World Bank Group in particular.[1]

The regionally oriented international development banks are of relatively recent origin. The oldest established is the Inter-American Development Bank (IDB), which came into existence in 1959 as an agency of the Organization of American States (OAS). It cannot really be classified as a true multilateral agency, however, as the basic political force which led to its creation was a desire on the part of the United States to strengthen its ties with Latin America. Its origins are reflected both in its status as an agency of the OAS and in the fact that the only rich country on its board of governors is the United States. Although a small amount of capital aid from other donors (Canada, Germany, Sweden, and the United Kingdom) is administered by the IDB, its prime functions are to channel both aid from the United States and commercially raised capital from the capital markets of several rich countries to Latin America.

The African Development Bank, established in the fall of 1964, cannot justifiably be described as a multilateral aid agency. There are no developed countries among its members who pay in capital. In addition, the developed countries have shown themselves extremely reluctant to channel any of their aid funds via the ADB unless the end use of the funds is deter-

[1] The phrase "the World Bank Group" is used to describe the International Bank for Reconstruction and Development and its subsidiaries.

Interested readers can find an excellent and exhaustive critical discussion of the operation of the Specialized Agencies in Sir Dudley Jackson's *Study of the Capacity of the United Nations Development System* (New York: United Nations, 1970).

mined in advance. Thus, so far at least, with uncommitted capital coming only from the African countries themselves, the ADB is not really in the aid business at all.

The Asian Development Bank comes closer to the model of a multilateral aid agency in that it receives most of its funds on concessional terms from donor countries and channels them to poor countries in the Asian region. It was established late in 1966 with a governing body composed of both rich countries (with roughly 65 percent of the voting power) and poor (Asian) countries (sharing the remaining 35 percent of the voting power). Although it receives the bulk of its finance from rich countries on concessional terms, the bank's own loan policy is more or less commercial. The (Japanese) president of the Bank justified [2] this approach on the grounds that "in the long run the creditworthiness, the efficacy and success of the A[sian]DB will depend on the extent to which it pursues sound development banking principles."

With one regional development bank primarily concerned with channeling funds from one donor, another channeling very little aid from rich countries, and the other operating with, basically, financial rather than developmental lending criteria, the only institution with a strong claim to be considered as a multilateral (capital) aid agency is the World Bank Group. Does this agency display the virtues claimed for multilateral agencies by their supporters? Beginning with a brief description of the operation of the World Bank Group, the next section shows how that agency is controlled and examines the realities behind the claims of independence and superior efficiency.

The World Bank Group [3]

The International Bank for Reconstruction and Development

[2] At a press conference in 1968, as quoted by John White in *Regional Development Banks* (London: ODI, 1970), page 64.

[3] This discussion of the World Bank Group is necessarily brief and selective. The reader is referred to the Suggestions for Further Reading, pages 169–173, for more information about it.

(IBRD, or World Bank) was established in 1945 as a result of the arrangements for the new international economic order drawn up by the Allied Powers at Bretton Woods in 1944. Initially, its operations were confined to financing the "reconstruction" of war-devastated Europe, with the first loans being made to countries such as France and the Netherlands. By the early 1950s, however, the Bank was specializing entirely in financing projects in the Third World. Although some of its funds come in grant form (subscriptions) from rich countries, it finds most of the finance for its operations in commercial capital markets and pays the going rate for it.

The Bank itself is confined to making loans for public-sector projects, but in 1956 it established a subsidiary—the International Finance Corporation (IFC)—with three objectives: the provision of risk capital for private enterprise in poor countries, the development of local capital markets there, and the stimulation of the flow of private capital from rich to poor countries. The lending and other operations of the Bank and IFC are carried out along more or less purely commercial lines. However, the awareness that the poorest of the less-developed countries are unable to meet the commercial loan criteria followed by the Bank led to the establishment in 1960 of the International Development Association (IDA) as another subsidiary. IDA is the "soft" loan agency of the World Bank Group and charges no interest on its loans,[4] which are generally made for 50 years (as against the 15 to 20 years of the Bank loans). IDA gets its finance in the form of grants from the rich countries, who collectively made commitments of $1,315 million to the association over the period 1967 to 1970.

Is the World Bank Group Independent of Donor Control?

The World Bank Group, like all the multilateral agencies, has no funds of its own but operates as an intermediary, transferring resources from taxpayers (and investors) in rich coun-

---

[4] It does make a service charge of .75 percent.

tries to (for the most part) governments in poor countries. Clearly, then, it depends on the political goodwill of the governments of rich countries to allocate tax revenues to it or to allow it access to their capital markets.

The only counterbalance to this effective financial control is diplomatic: as aid relationships are considered to be a relatively insignificant part of overall foreign policy, individual donors may not wish to antagonize countries whose alliance they seek. They may do this if they make major issues out of disagreements with the activities or policies of multilateral agencies. Indeed, visible and effective support of multilateral agencies has come to be a part of the overall foreign policy of many countries. There are, however, limits to the tolerance of donors, and they do from time to time criticize and censure multilateral agencies, sometimes to the point of withholding funds or limiting access to their capital markets. In addition, the agencies themselves impose limits on their activities and policies reflecting the fact that they do not wish to come into open and serious conflict with those people who control the source of their funds.

Without actually withholding funds or even threatening to do so, donor governments can play on multilateral agencies' instincts of self-preservation and their plans for expansion in order to prevent their activities from moving too far out of line with donor policies. Such influence is effected in many ways, from informal personal contact between officials of the agencies and representatives of donor governments to the outright determination of policy objectives in the governing bodies of the agencies. The former sort of influence can only be operational within the limits set by the latter. The degree to which these politically set operational limits "bite" depends on several factors, two of which are crucial. These are: the extent to which the desired limits are shared by the donors, and, second, the extent to which the donors wish to support the agency in question vis-à-vis other agencies or even at all. The limits which donors might wish to set on agency policies are primarily those concerning the overall amount of finance available to the agencies vis-à-vis their bilateral programs, the determination as to who should receive aid from the agencies, the determination of the conditions on which aid is extended, and the sort of purpose for which aid is made available. The recent increase in the flow of aid finance to the multilateral agencies reflects the opinion shared by most donor governments that international aid in general is a "good" thing, though individually they may have different reasons for holding that opinion. For some it is seen simply as a means of reducing the cost of maintaining a bilateral aid program, while for others it provides an opportunity to remove the link between specific aid flows and critical sections of domestic political forces. (They can still maintain the ability to influence, without publicity, the decisions of multilateral agencies concerning such flows.) One would predict, then, that given such reasoning, donors would tend to concentrate their aid resources on the agencies over which they had most effective control. This prediction is borne out by the facts: the agency most favored by donors in recent years has been the World Bank Group over which, vis-à-vis the United Nations agencies, they have most control.

The supreme organ of the World Bank Group is the Board of Governors, which meets once a year and consists of one governor and one alternate appointed by each member state. Effective day-to-day control of the World Bank Group is, however, delegated to twenty executive directors, five of whom are appointed by the five largest shareholders in the Bank (United States, United Kingdom, France, Federal Republic of Germany, and India), with the other fifteen being elected for two-year terms by Governors of groups of the other members. Voting, however, is based on size of subscription to the Bank's capital and the United States, United Kingdom, France, Germany, Canada, and Australia together account for more than half of the total voting power. The basis of voting strength in the World Bank Group contrasts with that in the United Nation system, where the one country-one vote principle is followed.

Voting strength is not, however, the only source of control

over multilateral agencies. A rich country can effectively control such agencies by withholding its subscriptions or refusing them access to its capital market. Thus, although the United States has had to accept the fact that United Nations agencies provide aid to Cuba in contradiction to its own policy toward that country, it has refused to increase significantly its contribution to the United Nations budget. In the case of one United Nations agency—the International Labor Organization—it has withheld its contribution completely because it felt the policies of that organization had become too socialist in orientation. The World Bank Group has not completely escaped such treatment. For several years France threatened to withdraw its subscription to the International Development Association (IDA) unless and until it allocated more of its funds to African countries which were once colonies of France. Similarly, from 1970 to 1972 the U.S. Congress delayed approval for funds for IDA, as it did not feel that IDA lending policies were sufficiently consistent with U.S. interests.

It is consistent with the basic thesis of this book—that the prime motive for aid is self-interest—that donor governments should channel their aid funds via those institutions which seem to them to be most likely to further their interests and appear to do it most efficiently. In the present international climate there are diplomatic gains to be had from being seen to support multilateral agencies, such support being currently politically fashionable. There is the important additional advantage that funds so channeled are, to some extent, removed from domestic politics while, for the major donors at least, remaining (to a large extent) within the control of their governments. In the national political framework governments have to justify and answer for each single item of expenditure of aid funds. Funds channeled internationally may be used to achieve the same purposes, while governments can dissociate themselves publicly from specific allocations which may attract disfavor in domestic political circles. Thus, in the United States, Congress may prevent bilateral funds from being used to support the policies of a regime in a less-developed country which the Administration and Executive believe should be supported; such support can be achieved via the multilateral agencies without the U.S. government being held responsible or being directly involved in the affairs of the recipient.

To the extent to which donors believe that they can insure that the objectives of the agencies coincide with their own, they will tend to concentrate their resources on those multilateral agencies over which they have most control. We have seen above that the agency over which donors have most control is the World Bank Group, and it is this agency which they have favored and which now administers the largest international aid flow. The favor in which the World Bank Group is held is reflected in the fact that its pattern of distribution of aid among recipients, its methods of operation, the conditions it imposes on recipients, and the purposes for which it allocates aid come closer to those of the bilateral aid programs of the donors than do those of any other multilateral agency. It is this resemblance which gives rise to the claim among donors that the World Bank Group is more efficient than any other agency, for efficiency is obviously relative to the objectives and methods of achieving them, and donors have faith in their own programs.

Is the World Bank Group Free from Political Controversy?

We have already noted the argument that by channeling more of their aid funds via multilateral agencies donor governments can divert domestic political attention away from some aspects of their foreign policy. But multilateral agencies cannot be politically neutral vis-à-vis domestic interest groups and lobbies. As they become a more important element in the total aid process, both in absolute terms and relative to bilateral programs, and are seen to be backed by incumbent donor governments, they will be assured of attracting critical attention from those governments' domestic political opponents. Comments from radicals such as: "The World Bank is now emerging as the pivotal institution for co-ordinating the expansion of American capitalism in the world economy"[5] are increasingly matched by comments from conservatives that the increasing importance of the Bank reduces the direct dependency of poor countries on donors. Liberals, too, are beginning to worry that the Bank (and other international agencies) are not sufficiently visibly accountable to taxpayers in donor countries concerning the use of their funds.

The period of vigorous expansion and transformation of the operations of the Bank Group inaugurated by its president, Robert McNamara, in 1968, has intensified the critical awareness of its activities maintained by both pro-aid and antiaid groups in all donor countries. Thus, the Bank Group can no longer claim to be free from political controversy. For example, the Overseas Development Institute of London, a pro-aid organization, said in its annual Development Review for 1972: "despite the new progressive image of the Bank under Robert McNamara, it has not lost its reputation for inflexibility, even arrogance. If the rather rigid control that the Bank exerts over the projects to which it lends is extended to sectional or national policies once it moves to program lending, the new approach may prove to be either ineffective or unacceptable to both recipients and other donors."[6]

Although multilateral agencies cannot have foreign policies of their own in the sense of seeking to further a single national interest, as their purpose is to provide assistance to specific poor countries they are likely, from time to time, to engage in activities which conflict with the national foreign policies of those countries which control them. If such activities were to conflict with donors' national policies too frequently, the agencies would cease to exist, at least in their present form. Thus, although the World Bank Group does not have a foreign policy of its own, its

[5] *International Dependency in the 1970s: How America Underdevelops the World.* A report published by the Africa Research Group (Washington, D.C., 1970), page 28.
[6] *Review 5* (London: ODI, 1972), page 16.

activities must be consistent with the foreign policies of the most powerful group of its members—the donor countries. The sole *raison d'être* of multilateral aid agencies is to act as a middleman between rich and poor countries, transferring resources from the former to the latter; and they will be supported only so long as they are felt by both sides to be operating in their mutual interest. In the donors' case this interest will be defined by the extent to which the activities of the agencies are consistent with the objectives outlined as goals by the donors when they set up their aid programs. For recipient governments, the interest is in having the agencies provide the resources they need to achieve their domestic objectives at a lower cost—both financial and political—than that at which they could obtain them from bilateral sources.

Is the World Bank Group More Efficient Than Other Aid Agencies?

The claim that the World Bank Group, or any other multilateral aid agency, is free from donor control and from involvement in the domestic politics of donor countries must be dismissed. Turning to the claim of superior efficiency and recalling that efficiency must be seen as being relative to the achievement of objectives, we can see immediately that unless the objectives of donor, agency, and recipient coincide, there is considerable scope for disagreement as to whether an agency is operating efficiently. At various points in this book it has been argued that it is difficult to pinpoint the development objectives of either recipient or donor governments. Consequently, unless the claim of efficiency is based on the objectives of the agencies themselves, it is difficult to see what the term "efficiency" can mean.

Unfortunately, we run into difficulties if we try to look beyond the simple mechanics of the activities of the World Bank Group over the years and identify the rationale of those activities. Thus, when Mr. McNamara said, "our goals [for the period 1969–1973] included trebling lending in the field of education, and quadrupling it in the agricultural sector," [7] he did not mean that the ultimate *objective* of the Bank Group was simply to increase lending or even simply to increase literacy and expand agricultural output. In the same speech Mr. McNamara said he believed that the Bank Group has a mandate to assist and "that assistance must be both in the form of the policy advice leading to sound social and economic development programs . . . and an augmented capacity to provide financial support for those programs." "In the end," he continued,

> development is like life itself: complex. The danger is to over-simplify. Development has for too long been expressed in terms of growth of output. There is now emerging the awareness that the availability of work, the distribution of income, and the quality of life are equally important measures of development . . . It is toward this broader concept of the entire development process that the World Bank is moving.

Mr. McNamara's statement, expressed in terms of objectives such as "availability of work," "income distribution," and the "quality of life," does not imply that the Bank Group *knows* how to achieve such objectives. No Bank Group official in the whole history of that agency would have said he advocated unsound policies or was unconcerned with employment, income distribution, or the quality of life. Indeed, over the years, the advice tendered by the Bank to its poor clients has varied in, for example, its sectoral emphasis, quite substantially. It is *possible*, though highly unlikely, that all such advice has moved the recipients toward a more efficient achievement of social and economic development. It is *unlikely* because nobody knows what price a society is prepared to pay to achieve full employment, what structure of income distribution it wishes to have, or in what terms it measures the quality of life. In short, there is no such unique thing as development. It is a process which can vary from country to country and from time to time, and

---

[7] This and the following quotations are taken from Mr. McNamara's Address to the Board of Governors of the World Bank Group, September 1971. Published by the IBRD, Washington, D.C., 1971.

the various forms it can take will be regarded in different ways by different people. One man's meat is another man's poison, and only the consumer can tell which.

No multilateral (or bilateral) agency can possibly approach all the inhabitants of the Third World and take a (nationally segregated) survey of what the majority of them would regard as criteria for "sound social and economic development." An agency has only two options open to it. It can either take without question the programs of the governments of the poor countries, assume that they reflect the wishes of their peoples, and help in their achievement. Or it can set up its own criteria of soundness and efficiency and attempt, in one way or another, to impose them on recipient governments by making its aid conditional on their acceptance. The World Bank Group for the most part does the latter, although its criteria do change from time to time. Whatever the criteria, however, our knowledge of the actual processes involved in social and economic change is such that no one can state beyond doubt that any particular program or set of policies is the most efficient way of satisfying them. Thus, the claims of efficiency made on behalf of the World Bank Group represent a statement of faith, a belief that those criteria used by the Group at any time are the "soundest" available which, again, given our ignorance of the nature of development, simpy reflects the fact that the claimant has the same prejudices as the Bank Group.

One area in which the Bank Group is generally recognized to be most efficient is in the evaluation of the viability of projects proposed for financing, or of the overall creditworthiness of an applicant country. In its dealings with poor countries the Bank Group performs two basic functions: it lends money to finance specific projects proposed by the recipients, and it advises groups (called Aid Groups or Consortia) of donors on the co-ordination of their aid programs to specific recipients. To perform these functions the Bank Group assesses the "soundness" of the projects (or other proposed expenditures) proposed to it for financing; it also assesses the "soundness" of the overall

economic policy framework of the recipient governments insofar as it affects the environment within which Bank Group-fi-
nanced projects operate and the general creditworthiness (i.e.
ability to repay aid loans) of the country. The import of previous paragraphs is that such criteria of "soundness" are necessarily
arbitrary. The advantages the Bank Group has over other agencies
and bilateral donors derive from the fact that it has a fairly narrow range of functions and can apply its chosen criteria on a
consistent basis, thus minimizing possible inefficiencies due to
different criteria being applied to different activities and different countries.

Even though its decisions on which countries to aid and to
what extent may be relatively free from restrictions, such as
meeting political or defense needs of specific donors, insuring
that aid-financed purchases are made from specific countries, or
that the staff on a project is drawn from one donor, the restricted
criteria it does use contain the seeds of conflicts between itself
and poor-country supplicants. Clearly, projects which a country
submits for financing or economic policies it has adopted have
passed some recipient-determined test of soundness; they may
not satisfy the Bank's criteria. It has been stressed throughout
this book that as there is no unique concept of development
there can be no unambiguous set of policies which can be defined as sound or efficient. When the Bank applies its criteria to
evaluate recipients' projects or policies only three outcomes are
possible: first, the criteria used by the Bank may be accepted
by the recipient, in which case there is no conflict and no problem; second, the criteria used by the Bank and those used by
the recipient may be so different as to be irreconcilable, in which
case either the recipient will refuse to accept Bank aid on the
Bank's terms or the Bank will refuse to lend money to the recipient
on the recipient's terms; and third, a compromise may be possible.

A genuine compromise solution can only occur if at least one
side to the negotiations regards the criteria of soundness of the
other side as sufficiently close to its own to allow it to modify its
own criteria without much loss of efficiency and prestige. A mock

compromise can be achieved if a recipient pays lip service to the Bank's criteria with the intention of following its own when the finance has been received. The extent to which it can follow such a course successfully will depend on how far it can attribute its switch in policies to forces which the Bank can be convinced were "beyond its control." A forced compromise may result either if a recipient feels so desperately in need of foreign exchange reserves that it is willing to accept the Bank's criteria even though it does not agree with them or if the Bank feels compelled to satisfy the political requirements of some of its Governors, even if this involves making loans for projects or to countries whose economic policies it considers unsound.

Conclusion

Controversy over the nature and extent of donor control over the distribution and use of aid will continue as long as aid programs continue to exist, regardless of their forms and institutional arrangements. All aid funds are derived from the tax revenues of the rich countries, and politicians in those countries will always attempt to insure that aid monies are used wisely —i.e. in ways consistent with donors' national interests. The arguments in favor of channeling an increasing proportion of the total aid flow via multilateral agencies have, however, proved persuasive. They would not have proved persuasive to politicians in donor countries unless the politicians had been convinced that multilateral agencies themselves operate in ways consistent with the objectives of donors. Such conviction naturally increases with the degree of institutional control donors have over the operation of the various multilateral agencies. As the degree of donor control over an agency increases, so does the disapproval of those who favor multilateralization of aid on the grounds that such control should be minimized. It follows that the agency (the World Bank Group) most approved by those who favor donor control over aid flows should be that most criticized by those who favor the reduction or removal of donor control.

One commentator captured the essence of the World Bank Group's dilemma when he wrote:

> Multilateral agencies stand in the middle ground between [rich and poor] countries. Aid is given on the basis of a rather loose assumption that the development of the world's poorer countries is in the long-term interests of richer and poorer alike. While this may be generally so, it is most unlikely, in fact plainly not the case, that the interests of rich countries and poor countries invariably coincide. . . . A multilateral agency is essentially a point of attraction, around which existing forces may be arranged in a systematic pattern. Its role is to balance these forces, tilting, where necessary, towards advocacy of the weaker force.[8]

If the Bank Group leans too far toward advocacy of the interests of the poor countries, it runs into the danger of a clash with those who control it; and if it leans too far the other way, it runs the risk of being regarded as a vehicle for the transport of donor policies to less-developed countries, thereby losing the prestige and support it commands in the latter. Both opinions are already to be found among minorities in both rich and poor countries. In rich countries criticism of the World Bank Group is being heard more frequently, and poor countries are trying to reduce their dependency on it. While multilateral agencies are undoubtedly free of some of the problems faced by bilateral agencies, there are problems from which they cannot escape. These derive from the nature of the business in which they are engaged and from their position in it.

[8] John White in *Regional Development Banks* (London: ODI, 1970), page 17.

VIII

WHO SHOULD RECEIVE AID?

Unanswerable Questions

In earlier chapters I referred to the concepts of "motives for giving aid," "need for aid," and "ability to use aid wisely in order to achieve sound social and economic development." I pointed out the impossibility of interpreting unambiguously such abstract notions in terms of practical rules for the formulation and implementation of aid policies. We saw that different donor countries and different groups within them have different motives for supporting aid programs. We saw how often these motives cannot be quantifiably related to aid flows, and how, consequently, it is impossible to evolve criteria to determine the distribution of aid. We saw also how it is impossible to decide how much aid individual poor countries "need," and, thus, why it is impossible to draw up criteria for its distribution according to need. And we saw that there are no unique quantifiable definitions of "wisdom," "soundness," and even "development" which might allow donors to decide which poor countries to support with aid.

After many years of being professionally confronted by such a complex problem, it is hardly surprising that the chairman of the Development Assistance Committee (DAC) of the OECD should exclaim, almost in despair it seems, that in order "to make a policy of true partnership in development work between countries with strong nationalistic tendencies on both sides of the table, *it will be necessary* to reach a *better* mutual agreement than now exists on criteria for the distribution of aid funds." [1] Faced with impossible situations, people tend to come up with impossible solutions; the chairman of DAC is no exception to this. His initial reaction to the problem which he set himself to solve was to write, "At first glance, it would appear obvious that the guiding principle should be to give aid more generously where it will produce the most development." He continued, however, by noting "the application of this apparently sound idea runs into a number of difficulties." Although to my mind he minimizes those difficulties, it is worth quoting them at length in order to see how the problem appears to somebody who is most closely concerned with it. He listed six basic difficulties:

a. Is it acceptable from a humanitarian viewpoint to reduce aid to the "least-developed" of the developing countries—those with per capita incomes under $100 and illiteracy of over 75 per cent for example—in which aid cannot hope to produce significant measurable development for many years?

b. At the other end of the spectrum should aid be concentrated on countries blessed with abundant natural resources and thus able with relatively little help to develop rapidly?

c. If one chooses a middle ground and gives most generously to countries making the best use of what resources they have, is "best" to be measured in terms of economic growth, social equity, political participation, or constructive international attitudes, or if all four, with what weight to be given to each?

d. Even evaluating just economic self-help, different countries have grown well with quite different patterns of exports, savings, investment, economic structures etc., and how is one to guess which will do well over the next five years?

e. Or is five years long enough to try to forecast whether a proper balance has been found between investments in human and material infrastructures or between them and quick yielding industries?

[1] Annual Report by Chairman Edwin M. Martin of DAC. *1970 Review, Development Assistance* (Paris: OECD, 1970), p. 26. My emphasis.

f. Looking at society broadly, is it enough that the government has advocated or even enacted sound measures or must the people also support by their daily actions a national commitment to development?
How can one measure this? [2]

The chairman of the DAC does not attempt to provide answers to these questions. Instead, he calls for an increased reliance on "the objective judgments of experienced people who can blend together value factors," and hopefully claims that such people could "hardly fail to improve present results." He does not indicate how such people would be identified or what institutional basis they should have, but he implies that they should play an important role in a dialogue between donor countries and individual recipients. This dialogue would provide a framework within which "past efforts and future intentions [of recipients] could be reviewed and an opportunity provided for at least a rough-and-ready inter-country comparison of self-help efforts, development prospects and need urgencies," an impressive job description for the "experienced people." The chairman added that if this dialogue was to be "truly effective both parties must be ready to change their original intentions. In the final showdown, recipients must be prepared to reject aid for low priority projects and donors to withdraw offers *if it is clear* their help will not form part of a *sensible* development effort."

In a fundamental sense the basic problems of aid derive from the fact that there is no simple answer to any of the questions raised by the DAC chairman. There is no universally accepted definition, either of what constitutes a "sensible development effort" or of the sort of experience relevant and desirable for those professionally engaged in the aid business. It follows, then, that there can be no unequivocal criteria for determining the distribution of the aid available nor for the determination of whether or not disbursed aid has been used sensibly nor for the selection of people to operate the aid process efficiently.

[2] Ibid.

The Source of the Problem

It is worthwhile recalling here the conclusions of earlier chapters, for they explain why the determination of the allocation of the available aid resources is a problem and why the questions raised by the DAC chairman arise. In the first place, it was argued that because the source of most aid is the taxpayers of the rich countries, the amounts forthcoming are likely to be seriously limited. The losses incurred by taxpayers as a result of the increased taxes required to pay for aid bear far more heavily in their minds than do the long-run, perhaps nebulous, benefits claimed to accrue from aid by their political leaders and pro-aid lobbies. In this situation it is obvious that politicians seeking electoral support will, in general, place less emphasis in their programs on the extension and increase of aid than on other policies which have greater electoral popularity. In most situations politicians are likely simply to accede, within the limits of their concept of "acceptable tax burden," to the requests for aid funds made by their administrations and executives. The exceptional situations (as in 1971 in the United States) will arise when the policy objectives which the executive and administrative branches of government seek to further with aid funds are at variance with the legislators' assessment of the mood of their constituents.

The limits set to the supply of aid funds by the representatives of taxpayers and electors are confronted by a notionally unlimited demand for such funds by the recipient countries. The poor of the world could absorb the total existing wealth and current incomes of the rich countries, and they would still be relatively poor by comparison with contemporary standards of living in rich countries. If all the gold and foreign exchange reserves owned by the rich countries were invested now in India and managed to generate an income flow of around 10 percent, the income of the average Indian would only about double to the still-miserable level of about $175. To raise that average income to, say, around the level of the United Kingdom, if returns to investment could be maintained at 10 percent, funds of the order of one and a half *trillion* dollars would be required. But if we remember that the Indian population is constantly expanding and that the return to investment would fall much below 10 percent well before such investment levels were reached, then we begin to get some notion of the size of the problem confronting the world.

We could take lesser objectives, either those of the governments of rich countries in giving aid, such as the generation of sufficient "development" to satisfy the demands of poor peoples for an improvement in their lot and to encourage them to keep the peace, or those of the *governments* of poor countries in seeking aid, such as the maintenance of themselves in power. We could *assume* that aid can help attain such objectives in some measurable way, quantifiable as a rate of return, but even then, the level of aid required would still be far beyond what the governments and taxpayers of rich countries would be willing to supply. Thus, the truth of the matter is that the rich countries are on the one hand not *able* to supply all the aid which the poor countries could usefully employ. On the other hand they *will not* supply more than they can convince themselves is in their self-interest.

Current Determinants of the Distribution of Aid

In situations such as this, where the supply of a commodity falls far short of the effective demand for it, economists usually look to the price mechanism (the interest rate in this case), or some substitute for it, to allocate the supply of the commodity among those calling for it. Clearly, there can be no resort to such a purely economic rationing mechanism in the case of aid (though some people do advocate increasing reliance on it), as to do so would be to contradict the *prima facie* purpose of aid —that is, to provide sustenance and hope to the poor, those least able to pay. What then does determine the distribution of aid?

Why for example was the average annual aid per capita received over the period 1967–1969 by Laos $24, by the Falkland Islands $380, and by Paraguay $23, while India, Ethiopia, and Haiti received, per capita, only $2.03, $1.72, and $0.97, respectively? There is no simple answer to this question, though the data available do indicate some factors which may have influenced the distribution of aid.

If we take the data on per capita receipts (refer to Table 2–9) published by DAC, we find that over the period 1967–1969 only 31 (out of 127) countries received more than $16 per capita each year. Of these 31, 24 were colonies [3] for at least some of the period, and 5 had military pacts with donors (Malta, Israel, Jordan, Laos, and South Vietnam). Also of significance, and reflecting these special relationships, is the fact that while the overall ratio of bilateral to multilateral aid for all recipients was 6 to 1 over this period, for 22 of these 31 recipients the ratio was significantly greater. Similarly, if we rank the regions of the Third World by their per capita receipts of aid, we find that South Asia, which is indisputably the poorest region of the world, comes out low in the ranking. For bilateral aid the order of the ranking was Oceania, the Far East (reflecting the strategic interest of the United States in South Vietnam, Laos, Ryu-kyu, and Taiwan), Africa (reflecting past colonial interests), Central and South America, the Middle East, Europe,[4] and, last, South Asia. For multilateral aid the order was Central and South America, Europe, Oceania, Africa, the Middle East, South Asia, and the Far East (including Indonesia).

Ignoring the relatively insignificant case of Oceania (which receives only about 3 percent of total aid), we find that over the period 1967–1969 those countries which received most aid per capita were those in which donors had a special military interest, or were African or West Indian colonies or recent ex-colonies in which donors could expect their bilateral political, economic, or cultural interests to be cultivated best. Of the

---

[3] Or they had a dependent status similar to a colonial relationship.
[4] Cyprus, Gibraltar, Greece, Malta, Spain, Turkey, and Yugoslavia.

$1,354 million received by Africa over the three years, $966 million (over 70 percent) came from colonial or ex-colonial powers, representing around 40 percent of the latter's total aid. To be a poor citizen of mainland China, India, Pakistan, and Indonesia, who between them contain almost half of the world's population and by far the poorest half, qualified one (and still does) to receive the least aid.

Regardless of specific motives, in the absence of evidence to the contrary we have to assume that the distribution of aid reflects the desires of the donors. For bilateral donors we must assume, if the reasoning of this book is accepted, that the distribution of aid which they actually choose maximizes the benefits, however specified, they reap from such expenditures. For multilateral agencies we must conclude that the pattern of distribution of their aid resources reflects their own concepts of efficiency, "wisdom," and equity. Who is to say that the actual distribution of aid is "wrong" and on what grounds? In several places in this book I have implied that there is no objective measure of aid requirements, either in total for all less-developed countries or for specific less-developed countries. Let me now state this quite categorically: there is no objective, scientific way of calculating the aid requirement of any less-developed country or, therefore, of the aggregate of the requirements of each individual less-developed country. Every poor country could usefully employ all the aid it could conceivably obtain from all sources (assuming it was all in the form of *real* aid, i.e. outright grants). It follows then that there is no objective basis for criticisms of the existing distribution of aid: the donors pays their money and they takes their choice.

But people do criticize the existing distribution of aid; there is clearly an implied criticism of the existing pattern of aid distribution in the above discussion. There can be only two bases for such criticism: either the mistaken belief that there can be and are objective or scientific methods of calculating an optimum distribution of aid or simply the *belief* that aid *should* be distributed according to a different set of criteria—i.e. that favored by the critic.

Can There Be a Scientific Basis for Determining the Allocation of Aid?

The simple answer to the question posed in the title to this section is: No. As one commentator put it:

> As for the allocation of aid among countries there is simply no way, short-cut or otherwise, to avoid making judgments as to how much each *deserves* in terms of the fundamental objectives of the aid. The use of incomplete or inconsistent criteria only conceals the real bases for the decisions made. *It may be politic* to conceal the value judgments implicit in aid allocations but we fool ourselves if we think that such judgments are absent.[5]

The key words in this quotation are: "it may be politic." They are irrelevant in the real world to the extent that *bilateral* donors extend aid for political, economic self-interest, or military reasons and justify such aid in terms of such factors. However, in the face of international or domestic questioning and criticism many bilateral donors and all multilateral aid agencies occasionally seem to feel a need to justify their aid allocations on pseudoscientific grounds. Clearly, by their very nature multilateral agencies cannot have political, economic self-interest, or military motives for determining the allocation of the funds under their control (although they may and do reflect those of their member governments). They do, however, need to be seen to allocate their aid according to some seemingly objective criteria.

In response to the felt need for some objective criteria, some economists have suggested formulae for determining the aid requirements of individual less-developed countries. Some of these were discussed briefly in earlier chapters in connection with their application to all less-developed countries together as methods of calculating the total aid requirements of the Third World. Here we will examine two of the best-known methods in somewhat more detail.

[5] R. S. Eckaus, "Economic Criteria for Foreign Assistance," in J. Bhagwati and R. S. Eckaus, eds., *Foreign Aid* (London: Penguin Books, 1970), page 162. My emphasis.

Perhaps the best known "Method of Computing the Capital Inflow Requirements" of poor countries was published in 1961 by Professor Paul N. Rosenstein-Rodan of the Massachusetts Institute of Technology.[6] He produced the formula:

$$F = (kr - b) \, \Sigma \, Y + 5 \, Y_o \left[b - \frac{S_o}{Y_o} \right]$$

for estimating the aid requirements of individual countries over a five-year period. In layman's language the formula [7] says that the amount of aid a country requires equals the difference between the investment requirements of the development program and the amount of investment resources available from domestic sources. (Strictly speaking, the formula calculates total foreign capital requirements—that is, aid plus foreign investment—but in the circles where the formula held sway, such investment is regarded as equivalent to aid.) The formula seems reasonable enough until it is realized that every country in the world, including donors, could apply it to its own economy and come to the conclusion that it required aid. Obviously, not all countries can be recipients. The crux of the problem is that the values of the variables contained in the equation are either determined by government policy or arrived at by *somebody* exercising his *judgment*, and some of the variables are impossible to estimate with statistical accuracy.

The Rosenstein-Rodan formula is particularly sensitive to the values given to four key variables: the level of income at the beginning of the five-year period, the average propensity of the community to save out of its income, the amount of new capital required to generate a given rate of income flow, and the rate of growth of income *it is assumed* that the economy can maintain over the five-year period. I will consider each of these

[6] P. N. Rosenstein-Rodan, "International Aid for Underdeveloped Countries" in J. Bhagwati and R. S. Eckaus, eds., *Foreign Aid*, page 81.

[7] In the formula the letter F stands for foreign capital inflow, k for the capital-output ratio, r for the rate of growth of Gross National Product which is denoted by Y, b stands for the marginal saving rate, S represents total savings, and the subscript o represents the value of the variable in the first year.

sources of difficulties in turn. The difficulties involved in accurately measuring the total income of any country in general and of less-developed countries in particular are well known. Even Rosenstein-Rodan admits, "In view of the nature of the statistical information available the margin of error in our computations may be estimated at ± 25 percent"! With the means of checking the accuracy of national income data being limited and dubious, it is obviously in the interests of specific recipients to inflate the figures representing the level of income the recipient hopes to support. Many readers will wonder why such a seemingly irrelevant statistic as the initial level of income should figure in the calculations at all. It does so because of the purpose assumed for aid by the deviser of the formula. Rosenstein-Rodan claims, "The function of outside capital (aid) in a development program is not directly to raise standards of living in the recipient countries but to permit them to make the transition from economic stagnation to self-sustaining economic growth." [8] For those concerned with the alleviation of poverty in poor countries the overall level of income is irrelevant data; it is important information, however, for those concerned with the mechanistic operation of raising an economy to the point of self-sustaining growth, a process which does not necessarily affect the lot of the poor at all. Indeed, it may worsen their condition, as was pointed out in Chapter 5.

The second key variable in the Rosenstein-Rodan formula is the average propensity to save. This propensity is a function of many factors. For example, it depends on the distribution of income, the prevailing tax structure, the rate of inflation, the incentive facing income earners encouraging them to save, and the relationship between the government's income and expenditure. All these factors are, to a greater or lesser extent, determined directly or indirectly by government policy; thus, the government can *choose*, within broad limits, the average rate at which its economy saves. So if the formula were to be applied strictly by donors, it would be in the interests of recipients to use their

[8] P. N. Rosenstein-Rodan, op. cit., page 81.

policy instruments to *lower* the rate of saving in their economies in order to justify larger aid allocations.

The average rate of savings maintained by a poor country has come to be regarded, in aid circles, as a measure of a recipient's success in *mobilizing domestic resources* (a catch phrase among those involved in the aid business). This concept, of the mobilization of domestic resources, appeals to the puritanical element in donors; it is taken to be a measure of recipients' *self-help* (another catch phrase) efforts.

Rosenstein-Rodan himself illustrates this attitude perfectly when he writes, "The principal element in this transition [from stagnation to growth] must be the efforts that the citizens of the recipient countries themselves make to bring it about. . . . Thus the general aim of aid . . . is to provide in each underdeveloped country a positive incentive for maximum national effort to increase its rate of growth." [9] Nothing could be a more hideous distortion of the truth than the claim that, regardless of how hard a man works or how poor he is, he is making no effort toward the development of his country unless he saves.

A more telling weakness involved in reliance on data of savings propensities is that such data are well known to be the least reliable data of all; it cannot be measured with any degree of accuracy in most poor countries and, consequently, cannot be taken as a meaningful measure of anything, even savings. In many official circles, however, such "problems" are ignored; the United Nations has even gone so far as to produce tables ranking poor countries according to their development effort as measured by savings rates,[10] and considerable attention is given to data purporting to measure propensities to save. This leads to the paradoxical situation in which poor countries are encouraged to produce phony data claiming to represent relatively high rates of saving, in order to show that they are making a significant effort to develop themselves. But such high savings

[9] Ibid.
[10] See UNCTAD Document number TD/B/C.3/28, *Mobilization of Internal Resources by the Developing Countries* (Geneva: UNCTAD Secretariat, 1968).

rates, when incorporated in the Rosenstein-Rodan formula, would lead to *lower* allocations of aid! In summary, then, the available data on savings rates have almost no scientific meaning; in particular they cannot be said to measure, in any way whatsoever, a poor country's need for aid or its ability to use aid "usefully." There is no way at all of telling whether a given rate of savings indicates whether or not a country is making a serious attempt to mobilize its resources in order to further its economic and social development. Any claim that it does is pure, unscientific nonsense and means simply that somebody is making a value judgment based on faulty reasoning and doubtful data.

The element of personal judgment is even more apparent in connection with the third key element of the Rosenstein-Rodan formula: the relationships between net additions to capital and the income flows it generates—k in the formula. Thus, depending on what sort of income it is proposed to generate (for example, income from agricultural or manufacturing activities) and on what sort of technique it is proposed to use to generate this income, the ratio—in technical terms the capital/output ratio —can vary widely. Figures varying from 2 to 6 are not uncommon. Thus a country proposing to generate a given type of income, with a given technology which involves a capital output ratio of 6, will require three times as much capital to achieve a given rate of economic growth as a country operating with a ratio of 2. Similarly, a number of compositions of output and a variety of techniques could conceivably be reflected in the same capital/output ratio. In the formula, however, the higher the capital/output ratio, the greater will be the amount of aid called for, simply, that is, because someone has chosen a more capital-intensive method of development. The flow of income generated over a period by a given increase in investment of capital in a country says nothing at all about the economic and social welfare of the poor in that country during the period. For example, a flow of income may be generated by investing a given amount of capital in a factory using a lot of expensive equipment, imported raw materials, and only a few people to operate it. In this case only a few people benefit—the owners of the capital, foreign suppliers, and the small work force. It might be equally feasible to invest the same amount of capital to generate a larger income flow by providing new inputs to, say, a lot of small peasant farmers, enabling them to increase their outputs and, thus, their incomes. Until recently donors have, in fact, tended to prefer to provide aid for capital-intensive industries (or projects) in poor countries (in order to provide markets for donor exports of machinery, etc.); such investment may do little to enhance the welfare of the poor in the recipient countries.

For a variety of technical reasons nobody can predict with any degree of confidence how much income a given amount of necessarily heterogeneous capital investment will generate over a given period; to pretend to do so is to indulge in pseudoscientific mysticism. Nor can anyone predict precisely the quality and type of capital which will be required to achieve a given improvement in the economic and social conditions of the poor. If such calculations were possible, many of the problems of development would have disappeared. And yet, the capital/output ratio is the only real economic variable in the formula: those describing savings characteristics are behavioral, and those referring to income simply describe the result of a combination of behavioral characteristics, technological factors, and resource constraints. Predictive formulas based solely on such a weak economic concept as the capital/output ratio are poorly founded. They involve somebody in making judgments as to the future composition of output and as to the capital required to produce that output. In the present state of development of economics and econometrics, and given the quality of the available data, such judgments cannot be claimed to provide the basis for a scientific criterion for the allocation of aid.

Finally, the Rosenstein-Rodan formula incorporates a figure for the rate of economic growth (r) as a factor in the determination of aid requirements. Who is to choose the rate of growth to incorporate in the estimate of aid requirements? The higher the figure, the more aid will be required, so that to the extent that aid allocations are based on this formula or others similar to it, it will pay recipients to aim at the highest possible target rate of economic growth. If recipients are not to be trusted to be realistic in their estimates of the possible rate of economic growth their economies can sustain, then outside "experts" will have to be called in to make a judgment. And of the economic variables which economists have consistently failed to predict with any degree of accuracy, rates of economic growth are among those most frequently got wrong.

There is also the problem of causality: in the formula the rate of growth appears as one of the factors determining the aid requirements of the economy, yet aid provides resources which (partially) determine the rate of growth the economy can sustain. What actually happens in some aid negotiations is that recipients set target rates of growth of income with a given composition to be produced by a set technology and then mechanistically calculate the aid required to sustain that growth. Donors then decide whether or not they judge the targets to be feasible or attainable at a lower capital cost, and on the basis of such judgments and other considerations they make an offer of aid. The recipients then have to vary their targets in accordance with the amount of aid they have been allocated. Among the "other considerations" donors may take into account are factors governing the quality of life of the poorer sections of the recipient community; but the rates of economic, social, and political progress of the poorer sections of the community are not necessarily linked at all with the overall rate of growth of the total income of the community. In sum, then, the Rosenstein-Rodan formula is based on the value judgments that the main objective of poor countries *should be* to achieve self-sustained economic growth *as fast as possible* and that the aid made available by the rich countries *should be* concentrated on those poor countries which are likely to be able to move toward this objective *most quickly*. The reader will note that these notional objectives, as determinants of the distribution of aid, have no connection with the *relative* poverty of the countries in the Third World. It has been argued in several places in this book that if aid is directed toward improving the welfare of the poorest sections of the world community, then the effect of such aid on the growth rates of the poor countries will be incidental. No growth at all may result directly from aid which is given in the form of food and medicine to starving children. On the other hand, if a well-established industrial sector in a poor country is held back only because of a lack of skilled manpower or certain raw materials, then aid which provides such skills or materials may have an immediate and marked effect on the growth rate of the recipient economy. Rosenstein-Rodan's criterion, although couched in scientific terms is, then, purely arbitrary and only acceptable insofar as one accepts the value judgments on which it is based.

The other popular method of "scientifically" calculating the aid requirements of less-developed countries is by using the so-called two-gap model, which was discussed in Chapter 5. It is called the two-gap model because it argues that two distinct gaps may prevent a country from achieving its development objectives. Its protagonists argue that, on the one hand, the savings a country is able to generate fall short of the investment requirements of the program—this is the "savings gap." They then argue that, on the other hand, even if there is no savings gap (i.e. savings are adequate), there may be a gap between the import requirements of the development program and the country's capacity to import, that is, its net foreign exchange receipts; this is labeled the "foreign exchange gap." The supporters of this model argue that the larger of these two gaps prevailing in any country is a measure of that country's aid requirements. We have already in Chapter 5 looked at the model in connection with its use by UNCTAD to estimate the aid requirements of specific less-developed countries and of the Third World in general. Some of its deficiencies were noted there; it is also subject to the criticisms I have made of the Rosenstein-

Rodan formula, as it incorporates many of the same concepts, such as propensity to save, capital/output ratios, and target rates of growth.

The trouble is that neither the savings shortfall in most models nor the foreign exchange gap in the latter in any way whatsoever objectively measure a country's need for assistance; they do not provide a scientific criterion for allocating aid. These two models, and all other efforts to establish criteria for the allocation of aid, involve subjective judgments. There are a number of reasons why this is so; I will examine some of the more general ones. In the first case, because of the way in which objectives are implicitly or explicitly incorporated in the models, they force the users of the models to emphasize one factor (or a small number of factors) as having an overriding importance in the subjectively preferred development process. (Thus the two models discussed above give primary emphasis to capital and foreign exchange flows as *the* important factors, to the more or less complete neglect of other prerequisites of the various forms development can take). In the second case, at no point do the models relate the welfare needs or initial poverty situation to their calculations of aid requirements. Third, they do not take into account the different forms which aid can take and thus they fail to make the necessary allowances; in particular they do not allow for such forms of aid as consumption subsidies and technical assistance. Not only can such models not be used to determine scientifically *the* optimum allocation of aid; they cannot even be used as a basis for objective criticism of existing or proposed aid allocations because they are not in themselves objective.

Who, Then, Should Receive Aid?

As it has been argued that there cannot be an objective, scientific method for determining the optimum allocation of aid, the question in the title to this chapter should really read: Who should decide who should receive aid? This brings us back to the subject matter of the previous chapter, so that by combining the conclusions of that chapter with the arguments put forward so far in this we arrive at what is, in effect, the conclusion of the book: as there are no objective criteria which can be used to determine the allocation of aid, some people must, of necessity, be selected and called on to exercise their subjective judgment in determining how much (if any) aid should be made available, who should get it, in what forms, for what purposes, and on what terms. Aid funds come, for the most part, from tax revenue, and in democratic countries decisions as to the allocation of such funds are left to the judgment of the elected representatives of the people. Such representatives are answerable to the people for their decisions, so that if people feel that the wrong decisions are being made, they can inform their representatives of their views. And in democracies, if they feel strongly enough about it, the people can remove their representatives and replace them with people who will more closely reflect their views.

Now we come face to face with the fundamental problems of democracy: on the one hand, electors do not choose their representatives on the basis of their views on domestically insignificant issues; and on the other hand, unless representatives are informed of (or seek to be informed about) the views of their electorate on an issue, they will make decisions consistent with their own judgment. And, as we saw in an earlier chapter, among the political issues facing electorates in donor countries, decisions concerning aid are relatively insignificant. Very few people make their views on aid known to their representatives, and they, in turn, are thus left more or less free to use their own personal judgment in determining what to do about aid. Naturally enough, they tend to make decisions which they believe will be in the national interest of their own countries. Thus, the bilateral aid flowing from each donor will naturally tend to be allocated among recipients according to a pattern which is seen by the governments of each of the donor countries as maximizing the gains accruing to their country. Obviously, no government is going to allocate aid to recipients which it believes to be following policies which will be detrimental to the interests of the taxpayers who provided the aid, nor will it support any international agency which does so.

It is open to any citizen or group of citizens in donor countries to say that, for one reason or another, they believe that their national policy on aid is misguided or wrong. I, as a political animal and citizen of a donor country can make, for example, the following statements of belief: that the alleviation and removal of economic poverty, social distress, and political discrimination are the most urgent problems facing the world community today and that it is the responsibility of rich nations to do their utmost to make resources available to hasten their solution; that all economic aid should be genuine aid—that is, in grant form and free from restrictions on where it is to be spent; that the use of aid should be rigorously controlled in order to insure that only those in need benefit and that the maximum possible efficiency is achieved; that I do not care whether aid is given bilaterally or multilaterally as long as the agencies concerned follow the preceding rules and that bilateral programs are effectively coordinated and free from self-interest; that the rules governing the distribution and use of aid should be made explicit and open to discussion among all parties concerned; that where recipient governments are seen to be following policies all of which are detrimental to the welfare of the poorer sections of their communities, they should be removed, forcibly if necessary, and the opportunity given to the poor to seek the improvements in their lot which they desire; and that donor governments should seek to cooperate with responsible recipient governments, individually or collectively, in the business of promoting social and economic improvements, assisting where they are able but abstaining from the imposition of their own judgments where these are at variance with those of the recipient. Most readers will consider such beliefs naïve and utopian. They are clearly at odds with the opinions of those currently responsible for determining the nature of and implementation of current aid programs. Clearly, too, there is considerable scope for disagreement on what constitutes, for example, "utmost," "need," "efficiency," "self-interest," "parties concerned," "detrimental," "welfare," "opportunity," and "improvement."

I am free, however, to temper my ideals to the demands of political reality. I am able to take the existing aid effort and argue whenever, wherever, and to whoever I feel might be useful, the case for changes in it, if I consider such changes would constitute improvement—i.e. would bring the system closer to my ideal. Such a process of awareness, critical examination and argument, and the ideals on which it is based, constitutes my political economy of aid.

SUGGESTIONS

FOR FURTHER READING

General

Bhagwati, Jagdish and Eckaus, Richard S., eds. *Foreign Aid*. London: Penguin Books, 1970.

Gardner, Richard N. and Millikan, Max F., eds. *The Global Partnership: International Agencies and Economic Development*. New York: Frederick A. Praeger, 1968.

Hawkins, E. K. *The Principles of Development Aid*. London: Penguin Books, 1970.

Mikesell, Raymond F. *The Economics of Foreign Aid*. London: Weidenfeld and Nicolson and Chicago: Aldine Publishing Company, 1968.

Ohlin, Goran. *Foreign Aid Policies Reconsidered*. Paris: Development Center of the Organization for Economic Cooperation and Development, 1966.

Pearson, Lester B. *Partners in Development: Report of the Commission on International Development*. New York: Frederick A. Praeger, 1969.

Peterson, Rudolph A. *U.S. Foreign Assistance in the 1970s: A New Approach*. Report to the President from the Task Force on International Development. Washington, D.C.: U.S. Government Printing Office, 1970.

Pincus, John. *Economic Aid and International Cost Sharing*. A Rand Corporation Research Study. Baltimore, Md.: The Johns Hopkins Press, 1965.

———. *Trade, Aid and Development: The Rich and Poor Nations*. New York: McGraw-Hill Book Company, 1967.

Ranis, Gustav, ed. *The Gap between Rich and Poor Nations*. Proceedings of a conference held by the International Economic Association. London: Macmillan and New York: St. Martin's Press, 1972.

Chapter II

THE STRUCTURE OF WESTERN AID PROGRAMS

Organization for Economic Cooperation and Development. *Development Assistance: Efforts and Policies of the Members of the Development Assistance Committee.* Paris, published annually.
———. *Flow of Financial Resources to Less-Developed Countries, 1961–1965.* Paris, 1967.
———. *Resources for the Developing World: Flow of Financial Resources to Less-Developed Countries, 1962–1968.* Paris, 1970.
White, John. "Fact and Fiction in Aid Statistics," *(South) Asian Review,* vol. 1, no. 3 (1968).

Chapter III

MOTIVES FOR GIVING AID

House of Commons, Session 1970–1971. *Report from the Select Committee on Overseas Aid.* London: Her Majesty's Stationery Office, March 1971.
Hunter, Robert E. *Development Assistance: Why Bother?* Washington, D.C.: Overseas Development Council, 1970.
Mikesell, Raymond F. *The Economics of Foreign Aid.* Chapter 1. London: Weidenfeld and Nicolson and Chicago: Aldine Publishing Company, 1968.
Nixon, Richard. *United States Foreign Policy for the 1970s, A New Strategy for Peace.* A report by the President to the Congress, February 18, 1970. United States Information Service.
Ohlin, Goran. *Foreign Aid Policies Reconsidered.* Paris: Development Center of the Organization for Economic Cooperation and Development, 1966.
Pearson, Lester B. *Partners in Development: Report of the Commission on International Development.* Chapter 1. New York: Frederick A. Praeger, 1969.
Peterson, Rudolph A. *U.S. Foreign Assistance in the 1970s: A New Approach.* Report to the President from the Task Force on International Development, 1970.
United States Senate, Foreign Assistance Legislation, Fiscal Year 1972. *Hearings before the Committee on Foreign Relations.* Washington, D.C.: U.S. Government Printing Office, 1971.

Chapter IV

THE DOMESTIC POLITICS OF AID

Africa Research Group. *International Dependency in the 1970s.* Cambridge, Mass.: Africa Research Group, 1970.

Geiger, Theodore. *The Conflicted Relationship: The West and the Transformation of Asia, Africa and Latin America.* New York: McGraw-Hill Book Company, 1967.

Goulet, Dennis and Hudson, Michael. *The Myth of Aid: The Hidden Agenda of the Development Reports.* New York: International Documentation on the Contemporary Church (IDOC) North America and Orbis Books, 1971.

Haslemere Group. *The Haslemere Declaration.* London: The Haslemere Committee, 1968.

Overseas Development Institute. *Annual Review.* London, published annually.

United States Senate, Foreign Assistance Legislation, Fiscal Year 1972. *Hearings before the Committee on Foreign Relations.* Washington, D.C.: U.S. Government Printing Office, 1971.

Chapter V

HOW MUCH AID IS NEEDED?

Pearson, Lester B. *Partners in Development: Report of the Commission on International Development.* Chapter 7. New York: Frederick A. Praeger, 1969.

Rosenstein-Rodan, P. N. "International Aid for Underdeveloped Countries," *Review of Economics and Statistics* 43 (1961): 107–138. This article also appears in Bhagwati and Eckaus, eds. *Foreign Aid.* London: Penguin Books, 1970.

UNCTAD Secretariat. *Trade Prospects and Capital Needs of Developing Countries.* New York: United Nations, 1968.

Chapter VI

CURRENT CONTROVERSIES CONCERNING THE FORMS OF AID

Bhagwati, Jagdish and Eckaus, Richard S., eds. *Foreign Aid.* Chapters 7, 8, 9, 11, and 12. London: Penguin Books, 1970.

International Bank for Reconstruction and Development. *Supplementary Financial Measures: A Study Requested by UNCTAD, 1964.* Washington, D.C., 1965.

Johnson, Harry G. *Economic Policies Toward Less-Developed*

Countries. Chapter 5. Washington, D.C.: The Brookings Institute, 1967.

Little, I. M. D. "Aid: Project, Programme and Procurement Tying." In H. B. Chenery et al., *Towards a Strategy for Development Cooperation.* Rotterdam: Rotterdam University Press, 1967.

Little, I. M. D. and Clifford, J. *International Aid.* London: Allen and Unwin and Chicago: Aldine Publishing Company, 1966.

Organization for Economic Cooperation and Development. *Development Assistance Committee. 1970 Review.* Paris, 1970.

UNCTAD Secretariat. *International Monetary System-Issues Relating to Development Finance and Trade of Developing Countries.* New York: United Nations, 1966.

White, John. *Pledged to Development.* London: Overseas Development Institute, 1967.

Chapter VII

THE MULTILATERAL/BILATERAL DEBATE

Hayter, Teresa. *Aid As Imperialism.* London: Penguin Books, 1971.

Hirschman, Albert O. *A Bias for Hope, Essays on Development and Latin America.* New Haven, Conn.: Yale University Press, 1971.

Krassowski, Andrzej. *The Aid Relationship.* London: Overseas Development Institute, 1968.

McNamara, Robert S. *Addresses to the Board of Governors of the World Bank Group.* Washington, D.C.: International Bank for Reconstruction and Development, 1970 and 1971.

Nelson, J. M. *Aid, Influence and Foreign Policy.* London: Macmillan, 1968.

Overseas Development Institute. *Effective Aid.* London: ODI, 1966.

Richards, J. H. *International Economic Institutions.* New York: Holt, Rinehart and Winston, Inc., 1970.

International Bank for Reconstruction and Development. *World Bank Group Annual Reports.* Washington, D.C., published annually.

White, John. *Pledged to Development.* London: Overseas Development Institute, 1967.

———. *Regional Development Banks.* London: Overseas Development Institute, 1970.

Chapter VIII

WHO SHOULD RECEIVE AID?

Chenery, Hollis B. and Strout, Alan M. "Foreign Economic Assistance and Economic Development" (Agency for International Development Discussion Paper, no. 7, Office of Program Coordination). Washington, D.C.: U.S. Department of State, 1965.

———. "Foreign Assistance and Economic Development," *American Economic Review* 56 (1966): 679–733.

Organization for Economic Cooperation and Development. *Development Assistance: Efforts and Policies of the Members of the Development Assistance Committee. 1969 Review.* Chapter 5. Paris, 1969.

———. *Flow of Financial Resources to Less-Developed Countries, 1961–1965.* Chapter 7. Paris, 1972.

Little, I. M. D. and Clifford, J. *International Aid.* London: Allen and Unwin and Chicago: Aldine Publishing Company, 1966.

Millikan, Max and Rostow, Walt W. *A Proposal: Key to an Effective Foreign Policy.* New York: Harper & Row, 1957.

"The Undoing of UNCTAD," *The Economist* (May 27, 1972).

UNCTAD Secretariat. *Trade Prospects and Capital Needs of Developing Countries.* New York: United Nations, 1968.

U.S. AID. *International Development and Humanitarian Assistance Act of 1971: Presentation to the Congress.* Washington, D.C., April 26, 1971.

INDEX

INDEX